HEART

OF A

CHAMPION

TRUE STORIES OF CHARACTER
AND FAITH FROM TODAY'S
MOST INSPIRING ATHLETES

STEVE RIACH

HARVEST HOUSE PUBLISHERS
EUGENE, OREGON

Cover by Jason Gabbert Design

Photos of Drew Brees, Paul Goldschmidt, David Johnson, Albert Pujols, Case Keenum, Dabo Swinney, Clint Dempsey, Dick and Rick Hoyt, Jordy Nelson, Jordan Spieth, Marcus Mariota, Benjamin Watson, Russell Wilson, Daniel Murphy, Carson Wentz, Derek Carr, Kirk Cousins, Tim Howard, Bubba Watson, Clayton Kershaw, Jason Witten © 2018 by Tom DiPace

Photos of Jenny Simpson, Kelly Clark, Brad Stevens, Simone Biles, Abbey D'Agostino, Monty Williams, Allyson Felix, Laurie Hernandez, Chris Paul, Kevin Durant, Jeremy Lin, Simone Manuel, Maya Moore, Steph Curry, Maya DiRado, Jrue Holiday, Lolo Jones, Kyle Korver © by USA TODAY Sports Images\ Part of the USA TODAY Network

Unless otherwise noted, all quotes appearing in this book are from personal interviews with the author or his team or from press conferences or other public media appearances by the featured subjects.

Heart of a Champion

Copyright © 2018 by SER Media
Published by Harvest House Publishers
Eugene, Oregon 97408
www.harvesthousepublishers.com

ISBN 978-0-7369-7282-6 (pbk.)
ISBN 978-0-7369-7283-3 (eBook)

Library of Congress Cataloging-in-Publication Data

Names: Riach, Steve author.
Title: Heart of a champion / Steve Riach.
Description: Eugene, Oregon : Harvest House Publishers, [2018]
Identifiers: LCCN 2018008254 (print) | LCCN 2018022321 (ebook) | ISBN 9780736972833 (ebook) | ISBN 9780736972826 (paperback)
Subjects: LCSH: Athletes—Biography. | Athletes—Conduct of life.
Classification: LCC GV697.A1 (ebook) | LCC GV697.A1 R49 2018 (print) | DDC 796.0922 [B]—dc23
LC record available at https://lccn.loc.gov/2018008254

Printed in the United States of America

20 21 22 23 24 25 26 / VP-CD / 10 9 8 7 6 5 4

"Sports do not build character; they reveal it."

JOHN WOODEN
LEGENDARY UCLA BASKETBALL COACH

CONTENTS

INTRODUCTION

The word "hero" is misused and overused in our culture. Dictionary .com (what happened to thumbing through the ten-pound *Merriam-Webster* version?) defines a hero as *a person noted for courageous acts or nobility of character; a person who, in the opinion of others, has special achievements, abilities, or personal qualities and is regarded as a role model or ideal; or the principal male character in a story, play, film, etc.*

Yet, as you read publications or online articles or watch the news, you find that the word "hero" gets tossed about like pennies into a fountain. Heroes, it seems, are a dime a dozen today.

Or are they?

What is it that makes a true hero? Ability? Achievements? Popularity? Power? Or is it something more intrinsic, something deeper?

I say it is.

Look back at the definition above. *Nobility of character…regarded as a role model or ideal.* Heroes are not characters, as the media would sometimes have us think. Rather, they are *people of character.* Good character. Men and women whom others admire and even want to follow because of their example of virtue and selflessness. Those who exhibit—no, embody—traits such as commitment, leadership, perseverance, teamwork, respect, integrity, responsibility, self-control, and compassion. These are true champions in my book. And, as you are reading my book…

These people are human, for sure. Fallible? You bet. Flawed and imperfect? Like us all. Yet something lies deep within them that makes them worthy of our admiration. They never give up, they treat people right, they live in integrity, and they use their platform to impact others. This describes the heart of a true champion…or maybe even a hero.

I've had the incredible privilege of telling the stories of these kinds of true champions for more than 30 years. I've been all over the U.S. and trekked to different countries to talk with them, observe them, and then tell their stories.

The men and women on the pages you are about to read exhibit the heart of a true champion. They have been acclaimed for their records, medals, and titles, and they have been considered among the best in the world at what they do. Yet each one lives for something greater, something bigger than themselves. As you read their stories, I hope you see what I have seen, and I hope you, too, are inspired to live for something greater.

I would love your comments. Reach out to me at www.steveriach.com or https://www.facebook.com/SteveERiach/.

Steve Riach

"Never doubt that a small group of thoughtful committed citizens can change the world; indeed it is the only thing that ever has."

—MARGARET MEAD

"To give anything less than your best is to sacrifice your gift."

STEVE PREFONTAINE

DREW BREES

»FACTOIDS

Drew was appointed by President Obama as cochair of the President's Council on Fitness, Sports, and Nutrition.

His book *Coming Back Stronger* made it to number three on the New York Times Best Sellers list.

I t's been said that, in sports, it's not the player's size that counts most. Rather, it's the size of that player's heart.

Drew Brees is the epitome of that maxim. Although some considered him to be too small to be an impact player in the National Football League, Brees is one of the most prolific passers in pro football history. Only two quarterbacks have thrown for more yards and touchdowns than the future Hall of Famer.

"He's not the biggest guy. He's not the strongest, or the fastest," said Brees's brother Reid. "But he'll still find a way to beat you."[1]

And this is what makes Brees so special. He has a competitive fire like few others. That drive has not only proved many experts wrong, but it also has sustained his success into his late thirties. He works harder than most athletes.

The New Orleans Saints star has passed for more than 70,000 yards and 488 touchdowns over his 17-year career through 2017.

He is third all-time in passing yards and, barring injury, should move into the number-one spot by week five of the 2018 season. He is tied for third in touchdown passes and should move into the second spot in 2018. His 6,222 completions rank second all-time, another mark he will surpass in 2018.

He has been selected to 11 Pro Bowls, has been named first-team All-Pro three times, and was the NFL Offensive Player of the Year in 2008 and 2011.

Brees has won at every level. In high school he led Austin (Texas) Westlake to the state title. At Purdue University, he took an underdog Boilermakers team to a Big 10 championship and a spot in the Rose Bowl in 2001, the school's first appearance at that game in 34 years. And in 2009 he led the Saints to the Super Bowl XLIV championship.

What is it that makes a winner? It's a question asked by every sports franchise in the world. They test and measure, run analytics, and spend millions of dollars trying to find the elusive answer. Yet the makeup of a winner is much more intangible than tangible. No one really knows how to find it. They just know how to spot it when they see it. And in Brees they see it.

"Drew is so committed as a player, that I think everyone in the building respects his work ethic and his commitment to our franchise," Saints coach Sean Payton told *Sports Spectrum* magazine. "He holds himself accountable to be prepared, both physically and mentally, and he sets the bar high for his teammates, and that is crucial to that position."[2]

While Brees may not have always looked the part of a pro quarterback prospect, he has always played the part. In fact, some have labeled him an overachiever. Yet that label doesn't do Brees justice. He may not have the big arm of some other quarterbacks, but his talent is undeniable. His talent and leadership have been recognized at every level.

He was the Texas offensive player of the year in high school and a two-time Heisman Trophy runner-up and Maxwell Award winner at Purdue, where he also was an Academic All-American and received a prestigious postgraduate scholarship from the National Football Foundation.

In the NFL, along with the aforementioned hardware, he's also received the Walter Payton Man of the Year Award and the Bart Starr Award.

"His work ethic is unlike anything I've ever seen," Reid said. "Even if he weren't in the NFL, he would still be a successful person."[3]

Brees's success on the field has been definitive. After being drafted by the San Diego Chargers in 2001, Brees persevered through some rocky seasons, most notably with a quarterback controversy and the Chargers using their number-one draft pick on Philip Rivers even while Brees was performing well as the starter. It seemed he still had to prove himself.

After leading the Chargers to the AFC West title and being named NFL Comeback Player of the Year, Brees still was not in the Chargers' long-term plans. At the end of the 2005 season, disaster struck: Brees tore his right labrum and rotator cuff while trying to recover a fumble.

"That was a real bad injury," said Brees. "It was my throwing shoulder, and it was potentially career ending. If you don't think for a split second, right after it happened, I didn't think, 'Why is this happening? Why me?'

"But I very quickly snapped out of it, and realized this is happening for a reason, and I'm going to turn this into a positive. He wouldn't let me face it if I couldn't handle it."

"He" meaning God. Brees became a Christian as a 17-year-old and realized a greater sense of peace and purpose.

"I accepted Jesus Christ in my heart and knew that there was something bigger planned for me than just sports," Brees said.

"From that moment on, with Jesus in my life, I knew that the fear of the unknown was there," Brees said in an interview during a live event at The Rock Church in San Diego. "With Jesus in my heart and in my life, I'm not afraid of the unknown. I'm not afraid to go to Purdue. I'm not afraid of dropping in the second round and being drafted by the San Diego Chargers. I know God has that plan and I'm going to trust Him. I'll be led by faith and not by sight."

Brees worked incessantly to come back from the 2005 injury. Most experts didn't believe he would be able to regain his arm strength after sustaining that type of damage to his throwing arm. Once again, Brees was underestimated. Once again, he did what others said he could not do.

In 2005 the Chargers, with Rivers in waiting, told Brees they weren't convinced he would fully recover. With his contract up, they made a less than desirable offer. Brees desperately wanted to stay in San Diego, but he saw the proverbial handwriting on the wall and walked. He was devastated.

"I said, 'This is the worst thing that has happened to me in my life,'" Brees recalled.

The Saints, however, viewed Brees as a star quarterback. They signed him, and in 2006 Brees led the league with 4,418 passing yards and guided New Orleans to the NFC South title and into the NFC Championship game.

"A year later," Brees said of parting with San Diego, "I looked back and said, 'That was probably the best thing that happened to me.'"

In 2007 Brees set the NFL record for the most pass completions in a single season with 440.

Two years later he led the Saints to a Super Bowl victory against the favored Indianapolis Colts. Brees tied a Super Bowl record with 32 completions and was named the game's MVP. It was also the first league championship for the Saints. In 2010 Brees was named *Sports Illustrated* Sportsman of the Year as well as the AP Male Athlete of the Year.

Since that pinnacle, Brees has maintained an amazing level of consistent excellence. Over his career he has had more than 400 completions in a season 9 times. He has thrown for more than 4,000 yards in a season 12 times. He has surpassed 5,000 yards 5 times, while no other quarterback in NFL history has done it more than once. He's had 9 seasons with more than 30 touchdown passes, throwing for more than 40 twice.

He holds NFL records for the highest single-season completion percentage at 72.0 and the highest career completion percentage at 66.9. He also holds the record for most consecutive games with a touchdown pass at 54 and tied the league record for most touchdown passes in a game with 7.

As accomplished as his career has been, Brees has valued his success off the field even more. He lives by an axiom that encompasses his four priorities: faith, family, football, and philanthropy. Brees likes to call them the "Four F's."

In 2003 Brees and his wife, Brittany, established the Brees Dream Foundation. Since then they have contributed more than $10 million to help advance cancer research, care for cancer patients, and assist with the building of schools, parks, playgrounds, and athletic fields in New Orleans, San Diego, and Purdue–West Lafayette, Indiana, communities. Brees worked extensively to help restore the city of New Orleans in the aftermath of Hurricane Katrina in 2005.

Brees is seen by the people of New Orleans as a local hero. They see his authenticity through the investment he has made in the community and because he and his family make their home in the city rather than in the suburbs. For Brees, it's about living out his purpose.

"I live for God, for the faith I have in Him," Brees said. "Knowing the sacrifices Jesus Christ made on the cross for me and feeling like it's in God's hands, all I have to do is just give my best, commit the rest to Him. Everything else is taken care of. That takes the weight off anybody's shoulders.

"God puts us in positions, all the time, for a reason. You can say, 'Why is this happening to me?' But you have to understand that it's happening for a reason."

PAUL GOLDSCHMIDT

»FACTOIDS

His great-grandmother sold candy door-to-door in Massachusetts after immigrating to the United States in the 1930s.

His favorite movie is *Billy Madison*.

He is one of the most devastating offensive weapons in baseball. Yet outside of Phoenix, few people are familiar with Paul Goldschmidt.

The Arizona Diamondbacks first baseman has been one of the National League's finest hitters since he entered the major leagues in 2011. Through 2017, over his first six seasons, Goldschmidt had a career .299 batting average, with 176 home runs and 627 RBI. He is a five-time All-Star and has finished in the top three in the NL MVP voting three times. He has won the Hank Aaron Award and the Silver Slugger Award (three times) for his hitting.

Tony La Russa, former Diamondbacks chief baseball officer, created a nickname for Goldschmidt: Albert P. Pujols.

The *P* stands for *Perfect*. Invoking the name of one of the game's all-time greatest hitters speaks for itself.

"I'm being honest," La Russa told *USA Today*. "Perfect. He works at every part of his game—defense, base running, hitting. He works to get better. He's a plus, plus player and a great teammate and he's dying to win."[1]

"The highest compliment I can give him is that he's so much like Albert Pujols that it's a credit to both of them," said La Russa, who managed the future Hall of Famer for 11 years in St. Louis.

"He's just a remarkable human being," Diamondbacks manager Torey

Lovullo told *Baseball Digest*. "You walk down the hall, security people, ushers, they feel the same way about him. You walk in the clubhouse, his teammates feel the same way about him.

"Now, I can get specific because I watch him perform and work every single day. I'm honored to be sitting in the same dugout as him. I still get giddy when he sits next to me and talks to me. I have to pinch myself and think, 'That's Paul Goldschmidt.' I'm just honored to be around him."

Even with Goldschmidt's growing reputation and his prodigious numbers, a disconnect remains between the public and those who watch him play every day.

"There's no part of his game that you're like, 'Well, if he did this better, he'd be a superstar,'" Arizona teammate Daniel Descalso said. "He does everything well, like no one I've ever really seen."[2]

"He's everything you want in a baseball player," said former Diamondbacks hitting coach and broadcaster Mark Grace, himself a three-time All-Star first baseman. "We know what a special, not only player, but a human being this guy is. He's not in a major market like New York or Chicago, L.A. or Boston, so he does get overlooked."[3]

It seems Goldschmidt has always been overlooked. He was lightly recruited out of high school and ended up at Texas State University. After his junior year he was drafted by the Diamondbacks in the eighth round and never showed up on any Top 100 prospects list during his time in the minor leagues.

Still, Goldschmidt could always hit, and he did so from the moment he became a pro. He batted .334 with 18 homers and 62 RBIs in 74 games of rookie ball in 2009, yet he was not satisfied.

"I remember him talking to the defensive coaches and saying, 'I want to be a Gold Glove first baseman,'" said Alan Zinter, a hitting instructor who worked with Goldschmidt in the minors. "This big, burly-looking, lumberjack guy with not the quickest of feet, not the best glove. It's almost like, Yeah, right."[4]

He made it to the majors, skipping Class AAA, less than two years after he was drafted. From there this once unheralded prospect has become a yearly MVP candidate and Triple Crown threat through determination and effort. Oh, and he did win a Gold Glove Award—actually three of them through 2017.

He also has studied the art of baserunning, and through his first six seasons has averaged 20 steals per year. He ranked seventh in the league in 2016 with 32 steals—a ridiculous number for a six-foot-three, 225-pound power-hitting first baseman who is known as one of the slowest players on the team.

"He's as good as it gets," Diamondbacks first base coach Dave McKay told *The Arizona Republic*. "Goldy is the type of guy who wants to be as good as he can get at whatever he's doing, whether it's playing first base or hitting or baserunning. If there's an edge and he can be better, then he is the one guy who seeks it out more than any player I've known."[5]

It's possible that the reason the player known as Goldy is overlooked now—even as the National League's best right-handed hitter—is because he is so humble. Self-promotion is not something reporters will hear from him.

"It was how I was taught to play the game," Goldschmidt said. "I can't control what people say about me. My focus is on what I can control and what I need to do to get better."

"His personality is just that. He doesn't seek the limelight," said Grace. "What he seeks is greatness. What he seeks is a world championship."[6]

"Sometimes I tell him, 'When you hit a home run, you need to do a little thing,'" said Diamondbacks outfielder David Peralta. "He says, 'No, I like to do the right thing,' which is good."[7]

"He'll hit a two-run homer and come in the dugout, and the first thing he does is tell whoever was on base, 'Good job, nice at bat, nice walk, way to be on base,' or something," said former Arizona teammate Josh Collmenter. "What he's doing is secondary to what everybody else is doing."

That old-school approach comes through in his approach to being on the field every day. Goldschmidt has missed just four games a year on average throughout his career.

"I always want to play and will play every game possible," said Goldschmidt. "My job is to play."

"He's come to the realization that he is the face of this team, the leader of this team, whether he wants to be or not," said former teammate Brad Ziegler. "If you asked him he would probably choose to be in the background and just go out and play. He doesn't want the limelight."[8]

"For a while now, professional players have been distracted by fame and fortune," La Russa told *Sports Illustrated*. "Which means that once you get some fame and you get some fortune—yeah, that's pretty good. You start sitting on the couch. When you see a guy that has just exemplary drive, if that's the word you want to use, it stands out. Goldy, he can't be better than he is."[9]

Interviewers often try to get Goldschmidt to open up and talk about himself. It rarely works.

"My personality is a little bit more of a shy personality," he said on a podcast of *The StewPod*. "I'm just doing my own thing. I can't really control what gets out there and gets written beyond my actions. So I share some stuff, but sometimes you want to keep some stuff private."

Goldschmidt's humility is matched by his sense of responsibility.

"I remember my dad sitting me down and saying, 'Hey, if you want to make the varsity team, you want to play in college, you want to play professionally, you've got to put in the work,'" he recalls. "You've got to show up early. You've got to hit extra. You've got to run extra. You've got to be in the weight room. I took that to heart and probably, at times, too much as I was growing up."

As evidence of how seriously he took that advice, Goldschmidt also had a 3.8 GPA in college as a finance major. Since he was drafted before his senior year, he determined to complete the requirements for his degree. In 2013, after taking a slew of online classes during the season, he graduated from the University of Phoenix with a degree in business management.

Goldschmidt's maturity comes from the keen balance he has achieved in his life.

"Your faith and your family are the No. 1 and No. 2 things in your life," he told azfamily.com. "Yeah, it's completely changed me."[10]

Goldschmidt's journey to faith is an interesting one. His father was Jewish, the grandson of parents who left Germany to escape the Holocaust. Goldschmidt's great-grandmother, Ilse Goldschmidt, was the heiress to one of the largest printing companies in Germany, but in 1938 she and her husband, Paul, and their five-year-old son, Ernie, fled the Nazis and reestablished their lives in Boston.

"They were living in Germany, and they figured out what was going to happen to them," Goldschmidt told MLB.com. "All three of them got out and were sponsored by someone. I don't know who."

While his father's side of the family is Jewish, Goldschmidt and his two younger brothers, Adam and Robert, adopted their mother's Christian faith.

Paul's mother, a Catholic, raised Goldschmidt in the church, but Paul said it never had meaning in his life and he developed a negative perception of Christianity.

"I had this thought, what I thought He [God] was like, what I thought the church was like, what I thought the Bible was like, or religion in general, that was not something I was attracted to," he said. "But then I realized I had this wrong picture in my head. So, I think that just opened my eyes and seeing teammates who were Christians...There was something different about them."

Goldschmidt points to former teammate Ian Kennedy, hitting coach Turner Ward, and coach Andy Green as among those who he saw a difference in.

"They showed me a lot of love," he explained. "That's the word I like to use. They cared about me as a person. They cared about my family and my wife. The way they treated people and the love they showed everyone and their openness was what touched my heart.

"It was a slow process, but I wanted to know more about these people. Why were they so full of grace and everything Jesus showed in his life?"

As part of the expression of his faith, Goldschmidt and his wife, Amy, have devoted themselves to outreach in the Phoenix community. They visit the Phoenix Children's Hospital so frequently they have badges that provide access whenever they like. Paul also speaks at numerous churches and events, sharing his story.

"I try to do as much as I can," he said, "but unfortunately we're all selfish at certain times, and I could do a better job of it."

That's just Goldy being Goldy. For him, there is always more to do.

DAVID JOHNSON

In the fall of 2016, football fans were asking, "Who is David Johnson? Where did he come from? And what makes him so good?"

By the summer of 2017, those same fans were making Johnson the first pick in their fantasy leagues (including yours truly).

The answer to "Who is David Johnson?" is simple. He's the top running back in the NFL.

Where he came from is also easy to answer. He played college ball at Northern Iowa.

What makes him so good is a bit harder to answer.

Johnson's success comes from a combination of athleticism, versatility, a commitment to excellence, and the drive birthed in him from being somewhat overlooked.

He made a grand entrance onto the NFL stage in 2015 after being drafted in the third round by the Arizona Cardinals. A highly productive backup during the first half of the season, Johnson started only five games as a rookie but still scored 12 touchdowns—8 rushing, 4 receiving—in helping Arizona reach the NFC Championship game. It was a harbinger of what was to come.

In 2017 he became the first player in NFL history to record 100 yards from scrimmage in the first 15 games of a season. He rushed for 1,239 yards and caught 80 passes for another 879 yards, giving him a league-leading 2,118 yards from scrimmage. He also scored a league-best 20 touchdowns. He earned Pro Bowl and first-team All-Pro honors.

"Running-wise, he's a mix of all the greats," said Cardinals offensive coordinator Harold Goodwin, who mentions Johnson in the same breath as Gale Sayers, Barry Sanders, Marshall Faulk, and Adrian Peterson.[1]

Stump Mitchell, who served as the Cardinals running backs coach during Johnson's first two years, elevates the conversation even higher.

"Listen," he said, "it's not far-fetched to think that David can be the best running back there is—or ever has been."

"I wouldn't trade him for anybody," said Cardinals general manager Steve Keim.[2] By this he means any player at any position in the entire NFL.

It wasn't always this way for Johnson. In fact, he was overlooked or marginalized most of his life before coming to Arizona. His childhood was spent running from things he wanted to forget.

Johnson's father abandoned him when he was little. His mother, Regina, struggled to raise her six children. She worked multiple jobs and moved several times, often finding shelter in cheap motels. Johnson spent most of his nights wondering where he would sleep while most of his days in the summer were devoted to working in the cornfields.

When Johnson was in grade school, his mother was jailed for driving under the influence, so he moved in with an older sister. When his mom was released, she quit drinking, but the lifestyle meant money was scarce. To make matters worse, Johnson became the target of a bully who stalked him constantly.

While it seems implausible that the well-built six-foot-one, 224-pounder could ever have been the victim of bullying, it's perhaps the most painful aspect of his childhood.

"I get that the most when I tell my story," Johnson told *Sports Illustrated*. "'There's no way you were bullied.' They didn't know I wasn't always this big. Sometimes they don't believe me, and I have to really tell my story, that I had to go through the same thing they have to go through."

The bully—a high schooler who was three or four years older—tormented Johnson after school. Once he took Johnson's winter hat from a basketball game at the local YMCA and told Johnson the hat was now his.

Another time the bully found Johnson at the Y and started beating up Johnson and his cousin. Johnson ran away, leaving his cousin alone to fight, a decision he still feels bad about.

The harassment was so painful, Johnson never told anyone about it. Now he does. Through his Mission 31 Foundation, he combats bullying at schools, sharing his story and encouraging students to be accepting of everyone. He also made bullying his focus, as displayed on his footwear when the NFL began its "My Cause, My Cleats" initiative.

"I want to talk about it," he said. "I feel like, with kids being bullied, I feel like if they have one friend, one kid they spoke to, that would change their lives."

Back then, with no one to talk to, Johnson was simmering under the surface, looking for an escape. He found it in football, where he liked to please his coaches and lose himself in the contact.

Johnson made varsity as a sophomore at Clinton High, where he scored 42 touchdowns as a senior.

Yet his diverse and advanced skill set made it difficult for college football recruiters to see him as a running back. Some coaches saw him as a linebacker, others as a defensive back. And some didn't even get his name right. Iowa State's letter to him was addressed to David *Jacobson*.

So Johnson went to Northern Iowa, where only a prophet would have been able to predict his success in the NFL.

Northern Iowa's coaches didn't know what to do with him, so they tried him at safety. Offensive coordinator Bill Salmon told him at one practice, "Intercept another pass, and you'll never play offense again."

The coaches moved Johnson to receiver and then had him play both receiver and running back.

Johnson learned how to run passing routes, fake out defensive backs, and make precision cuts. He put in substantial work in the weight room, improving his max squat from 470 pounds to 670 and his bench press from 275 to 435.

All the reps at receiver allowed Johnson to grow into his place at the running back position. Over the next four years he set UNI records for rushing yards (4,687), all-purpose yards (6,859), and touchdowns (64). He scored four times against Iowa State, the team that couldn't get his name right on their recruiting letter.

When Johnson was not working over opponents, he was working

at various jobs to support himself. He spent summers removing asbestos, working as a handyman, and earning nine dollars an hour cleaning campus toilets, installing blinds, repairing stoves, and unclogging shower drains.

"That's the stuff I had to do in the summer, whereas I think other college student-athletes were able to just work out," he said. "I had to do a job, and I had to work out at the same time, so I think that's really where I learned how to have my work ethic."

As the 2015 NFL draft approached, Johnson was determined to prove the doubters wrong, not just those from the NFL, but from his entire life.

When he arrived at the Senior Bowl, a Jacksonville Jaguars scout couldn't find his name on his list and asked, "Do you play linebacker?"

Another pro scout's take of Johnson before the draft was that "[he] lacks the short-area quickness to be a consistently effective every-down running back...Isn't a classic finisher."

Johnson took a picture of that report and read it multiple times each day.

The Cardinals drafted Johnson in the third round, after another running back they had targeted had already been chosen.

A few months later, in training camp, general manager Keim felt he may have stumbled onto greatness when he watched Johnson take a pitchout and blow through a hole in the defense like a sprinter. *A 224-pound human isn't supposed to move like that,* Keim thought to himself. He turned to those nearby and mouthed "Wow!"

As a rookie, Johnson scored the first time he touched the ball in his very first regular-season game, turning a short pass in the 2015 season opener into a 55-yard touchdown against the Saints. The next week, at Chicago, he returned the opening kickoff 108 yards for a score. The Pro Football Hall of Fame called after the game—they wanted his cleats.

That season Johnson became just the fourth rookie in NFL history to record 500 yards rushing, 400 receiving, and 500 in kickoff returns and to score at least 13 touchdowns.

In 2016 he broke more records and quickly became one of the elite backs in the NFL. As evidence of his freakish skill set, Johnson was rated as the top-graded wide receiver by Pro Football Focus for the 2016 season, even though he was a running back.

"Very few humans possess his background or his physical skill set," Keim told *Sports Illustrated*.[3]

In 2017 he set his sights on joining Roger Craig and Marshall Faulk as the only players ever to gain 1,000 yards rushing and receiving in the same season.

He cut fast food from his diet in the off-season and worked to improve his flexibility, muscle symmetry, and balance.

But a not-so-funny thing happened on the way to making history. Johnson dislocated his wrist in the first game of the 2017 season, had surgery, and missed the rest of the year.

"A weird injury and it's really not a common injury in football," said Johnson, who had never missed more than one game playing football at any level.

"At the beginning, it was very tough. I was down on myself. I was thinking, what could I have done on that play better, to change the play? Maybe my wrist wasn't strong enough."

The time off allowed him to be present for the major milestones of his son, David Jr., born to him and his wife Meghan in January 2017.

"When he rolled over I was there," Johnson said. "I was there when he started crawling. I need to be there, support him. I might not know what I'm doing, but just being there, learning from those mistakes and moments, supporting him. Being there at every developing milestone that he has."

Because of his son's impending birth, Johnson declined the invitation to the Pro Bowl that same month. It was a good decision. Meghan had numerous complications, including preeclampsia, a potentially serious blood-pressure disorder occurring in just 5 percent of U.S. women.

When David Jr. was born, the doctors let Johnson catch his son. His only thought: *Don't fumble.*

After the birth, David and Meghan retreated to their home outside Tempe. The house, like the man, is big but not fancy. The blinds stay drawn, and the Johnsons have their groceries delivered to maintain some privacy. Johnson is still adapting to the attention he receives.

He will receive more attention in the years ahead. After the 2017 season, star quarterback Carson Palmer announced his retirement and head coach Bruce Arians also stepped down. Suddenly, the Cardinals' window for success seemed much smaller, and that window will be in the hands of Johnson.

"I'm blessed, and I thank God for giving me this platform, for giving me the ability and the skill to play in this league," he said. "If it wasn't for Him, I wouldn't be where I am today.

"I think God is working on me right now as for being a leader. He's doing stuff to put me in positions to try to be a leader, but sometimes I get scared or I don't want to. I feel like I'm going to say the wrong thing to the team or do the wrong thing, and I feel like He keeps wanting to put me in those positions."

Johnson sees it as an opportunity to lead through his actions, actions he hopes will demonstrate who he truly is.

"Just the small things I've learned from the Bible, those small things go a long way in how I conduct myself," Johnson said. "People don't have to ask us if we are Christians. They know by the way we conduct ourselves, by the way we speak, and even by the way we play football."

*"Ability may get you to the top,
but it takes character to keep you there."*

JOHN WOODEN

ALBERT PUJOLS

»FACTOIDS

His nicknames are El Hombre, The Machine,
Prince Albert, Phat Albert.

On February 7, 2007, Pujols became a U.S. citizen,
scoring a perfect 100 on the citizenship test.

Albert Pujols is a sports anomaly, a rare athlete who immediately dominated his game at the professional level and then continued to perform at an elite level into two decades.

At the beginning of the 2000 season, Pujols was a first-year professional baseball player. As a 20-year-old aspiring star fresh out of junior college, he was toiling away in the minor league at Class-A Peoria (Illinois), hoping to make it big. By the end of 2001 he was runner-up as the National League's MVP. Fifteen years later he was a Hall of Famer in waiting.

Pujols made quite an entrance as a rookie for the St. Louis Cardinals in 2001, hitting .329 with 37 home runs, 130 RBIs, and 112 runs scored in what was one of the most remarkable rookie seasons in baseball history.

"He plays like a 30-year-old," then Cardinals manager Tony La Russa told the St. Louis press corps at the time.

Pujols was unanimously selected as the NL Rookie of the Year that year, and he finished fourth in the league's MVP voting.

Many around baseball wondered where Pujols had come from. Limited information on him as a prospect had circulated around baseball prior to his first season. Some were asking if his performance was a fluke.

To show he was no fluke, Pujols hit .314 with 34 homers, 127 RBIs, and 118 runs scored in his second season, and he placed second in the league's MVP vote.

A legend was born. Perhaps the quietest legend in sports history.

Through 2017, Pujols had put up numbers that have been matched by only a few in the history of the game. His 614 career home runs placed him seventh all-time and within two-years' striking distance of the top five. His 1,918 RBIs place him ninth all-time, with an opportunity to climb as high as fourth during the 2018 season. He also sat twelfth in doubles and fourteenth in slugging percentage. With 2,968 hits, he is certain to end up a member of the coveted 3,000 hit club.

The statistical run he had in St. Louis over his first seven seasons was at a level only achieved previously by the likes of Ted Williams, Babe Ruth, Lou Gehrig, and Jimmie Foxx.

In just his third year, in 2003, Pujols had one of the greatest individual seasons in Cardinals history, batting .359 with 43 home runs and 124 RBIs. He won the NL batting title and led the National League in runs, hits, doubles, extra base hits, and total bases. At the age of 23, he became the youngest NL batting champion since 1962, and he joined Hall of Famer Rogers Hornsby as the only players in Cardinals history to record 40 plus homers and 200 plus hits in the same season. He also had a 30-game hitting streak.

The following seasons saw similar greatness:

- 2004: .331, 46 home runs, and 123 RBIs, when he was also MVP of the NL Championship Series in helping the Cards reach the World Series, where they were defeated by the Boston Red Sox—all while Pujols was battling plantar fasciitis.

- 2005: .330, 41 home runs, 117 RBIs, 97 walks, and 16 stolen bases, while earning National League MVP honors. His 201 career home runs through five seasons trailed only Ralph Kiner for the most in baseball history over such a span.

- 2006: .331, 49 home runs, and 137 RBIs, while he again battled injuries. Pujols became the fastest ever to hit 250 career home runs, and he was voted to receive his first Gold Glove Award while helping the Cards win the World Series.

- 2007: He became the first player ever to hit at least 30 home runs in each of his first seven seasons, and the third player ever to drive in 100 or more runs in each of his first seven seasons (joining Ted Williams and Joe DiMaggio). He also became the only player in history to start his career with seven consecutive seasons with a .300 batting average, 30 HRs, 100 RBIs, and 99 runs scored.

The numbers continued through the seasons that followed, putting Pujols on equal footing with Cardinals legend Stan Musial as the most accomplished and beloved players in franchise history. Yet when his contract was up in 2012, Pujols went elsewhere. He had wanted to finish his career in St. Louis, but the Cardinals were not willing to offer a long-term deal. Pujols agonized over the decision and eventually chose to sign a ten-year, $240 million deal with the Los Angeles Angels.

While battling injuries constantly during his time in Anaheim, Pujols has remained one of the game's top run producers in the twilight of his career, blasting 169 homers and driving in more than 100 runs in four of his six seasons in Southern California.

In 2017 Pujols became the all-time leading home run hitter among foreign-born players, passing Sammy Sosa.

Those in baseball have recognized throughout Pujols's historic career that they have observed a baseball Rembrandt, one of the truly greats in the history of the sport.

"He's rare," said former Cardinals hitting instructor Mitchell Page. "You look at that [swing] and you think of names like Ted Williams, Rod Carew, and George Brett, guys with beautiful, pure swings. Swings like his don't happen very often. It's a gift."

Pujols's reputation as a hitting machine is paralleled only by his reputation as a true gentleman. So where did this man who seemed to step off the pages of a Chip Hilton novel come from? What made him so good? To understand both, one needs to go back to the early days of Albert Pujols's life, a life that never envisioned where he has ended up.

Born and raised in Santo Domingo, Dominican Republic, José Alberto Pujols Alcántara was the youngest of 12 children in a family that led a somewhat typical life in the impoverished baseball-loving country.

He did not have the privilege of growing up in a traditional family unit. His father, Bienvenido, was in and out of his life from early on, so Albert was raised mostly by his grandmother, whose name—America— foreshadowed what was to come.

His ten uncles and aunts seemed more like brothers and sisters to him in what was a close, extended family. They all lived together in a communal setting that resembled a campsite and would not have survived had it not been for government assistance programs.

Despite his meager surroundings, Albert grew up happy and well adjusted, due in great part to his grandmother. She treated him as her own son and passed along her religious beliefs and ethics.

Though Albert rarely saw his father, he knew he wanted to follow in Bienvenido's footsteps. The elder Pujols had been a great pitcher in the Dominican leagues. When he was a toddler, Albert gained his father's passion for baseball, and by age six he was playing the game every day on the dusty fields near his home. It was there the dream of one day being a major leaguer was birthed.

When Pujols was 16, his father decided to move to the United States and bring Albert with him. They settled in Independence, Missouri, just outside Kansas City, where Albert enrolled at Fort Osage High School and quickly became a baseball star. While he may not have had much of a grasp of American culture, the one thing young Albert had always been able to do was hit a baseball.

He became the most feared hitter in the area, batting .660 with eight home runs as a senior and being honored as a two-time All-State performer. He then went to Maple Woods Community College in Kansas City, where he hit .461 during his only season at the school.

Even with his potent bat, few Major League clubs showed interest. A Colorado Rockies scout filed a favorable report about the young hitter, but the club took no action. The Tampa Bay Rays gave Pujols a tryout, but it went poorly and the team did not draft him. Finally, in the thirteenth round of the 1999 draft, the Cardinals selected Albert with the 402nd overall pick. He initially turned down a $10,000 bonus offer and opted to play in the amateur Jayhawk League in Kansas. By the end of the summer of 1999, however, the Cardinals increased their bonus offer to $70,000, and Pujols signed.

For the remainder of the '99 season, Pujols played for the Single-A Peoria Chiefs of the Midwest League. In 2000 he shot through the ranks of the Cardinals farm teams, starting with the Potomac Cannons of the Class-A Carolina League and then being promoted to the Triple-A Memphis Redbirds by the end of the season.

After just one full season in the minor leagues, Pujols was invited to major league spring training in 2001. The Cardinals wanted to expose him to a big-league camp so as to groom him for the future. He played so well in the spring, however, the team could not break camp without adding him to the roster. So, at the age of 21 and with just one season of minor league baseball under his belt, Pujols began his major league career, comparing notes with the likes of Mark McGwire. When the Cardinals were hit with injuries, Pujols broke into the lineup, began smashing line drives, and a star was born.

Yet Pujols seems nonplussed over his historic numbers. To him, they simply represent past success. He has consistently remained keenly focused on what is next.

"All I'm thinking about is today," he said. "Going into spring training, you don't try to win the MVP. All you're going to do is help out your team to win. If you can do that, this is the reward that you get after the season.

"My goal is to win a World Series. That's it. I don't like to set many goals for myself. Focusing on a single goal relaxes you…Of course I'd take 40 homers, a .330 average, and 100 RBIs, but it can be better. I want to get better every year. I never want to be satisfied."

The intense desire to get better has driven Pujols to work harder each year. He is committed to squeeze every ounce of production out of his ability. For him, this means hours of preparation and work.

"Preparation is very important," he said. "The pitcher is going to do his job and prepare for you, so you as a hitter must do the same. I always watch videotape of pitchers before the game and even sometimes during."

At times this single-minded approach has made Albert come across as being too serious.

"I'm a grown man," he said. "People have always told me I act like I'm 50 years old. That's the way God made me, and that's the way I grew up. If I want anything, I just work at it harder."

That work ethic is just part of what has made Pujols a success. It would not have happened without the timely move to the States with his father. Nor could it have happened, Pujols said, without the perspective brought by his wife, Deidre, whom he met in 1998 and married on New Year's Day 2000.

At the start of their relationship, Deidre told Albert that her Christian faith was the foundation for her life. Soon Albert, who had only gone to church occasionally while growing up, decided to follow his wife's lead and become a Christian as well. The change gave him a profound sense of thankfulness and helped him keep perspective in the midst of his success.

"The Lord gave me this talent and ability to be in this position," Pujols said. "If it wasn't for Him, I don't think I would have been here today. Everything we have right now comes from the Lord. All the credit for the success I've had is going to Him, every single at bat.

"I'm trying to follow my Lord Jesus. That's who I'm trying to represent every day I step on the field when I cross the line. I know there are 35,000 to 45,000 people watching me play, but at the end I'm only playing for the Lord.

"I always say God doesn't need me, but I need Him in my life to survive in this world…Whatever we go through, the good times or the bad times, He's always going to be there for us."

Such perspective has also inspired in Pujols a desire to give back. In 2005 Albert and Deidre launched the Pujols Family Foundation to do just that. Pujols's mission, he said, is to live and share his commitment to faith, family, and others; to promote awareness; and to provide hope and meet the tangible needs of children and families who live with Down syndrome. The goal is also to improve the standard of living and quality of life for impoverished people in the Dominican Republic through education, medical relief, and tangible goods and to provide extraordinary experiences for children with disabilities and/or life-threatening illnesses.

Through the foundation, the Pujolses have impacted the lives of hundreds of children with Down syndrome in honor of their daughter, Isabella, who has the condition. They also support the Niños de Cristo Orphanage in the Dominican Republic—near the place of Albert's birth—to help the underprivileged in his home community.

"The Dominican Republic is a poor country," Pujols said, ever aware of his beginnings. "I asked God that if I ever got to play here, when I got the money, I wanted to help the country out. That's one of the main things. I want to help the country out."

To continue to do so, Pujols must keep working—and keep hitting—both which seem to come quite naturally to the six-foot-three, 225-pound slugger.

"When I walk out of this game…I want to be the best player I can be," Pujols said. "I want to be remembered as a dedicated worker who never got lazy. I want to be the same Albert Pujols…the same person no matter how much success I might have.

"I thank God for the incredible opportunity to play the game of baseball…My work on the field is always for something greater—to glorify God and to serve others."

"The difference between a successful person and others is not a lack of strength, not a lack of knowledge, but rather in a lack of will."

VINCE LOMBARDI

JENNY SIMPSON

Jenny Simpson is a woman on the run—always.

The American middle-distance champion lives life in a pair of running shoes. Actually several pairs of running shoes.

It seems Simpson has been in a hurry to see just how good she can be. In fact, it is her mission.

After setting the U.S. record in the 3,000-meter steeplechase, Simpson moved on to a new challenge. She quickly became an elite runner in middle-distance races, running both the 3,000 and 1,500 meters, and stopped competing in the steeplechase. In the 1,500, she became one of the best in the world.

Simpson has won three global medals at 1,500 meters: bronze at the 2016 Olympics, silver at the 2013 World Championships, and gold at the 2011 World Championships, where she became the best in the world at that distance.

It was her bronze at the 2016 Rio Olympic Games that seemed to show the world her talent and grit.

When Simpson won the bronze medal in Rio de Janeiro, she had finally run down the one accomplishment lacking from her impressive list of accolades. The World Championship gold in 2011 was a highlight, for sure, but this was the Olympics. It was also a first for the United States, which had never had a woman medal in this race at the Olympics until, that is, Simpson crossed the finish line. She did it by surging from sixth to third in the final 300 meters—200 of which she wouldn't even remember after the race.

"I just remember crossing the finish line ugly-crying," she said. "It is Everest. Getting to the top of this is so hard."

But she did it. This was a far cry from the 2012 London games, when, as the reigning world champion and favorite for the gold, she failed to qualify for the final.

"Four years ago, I didn't make the final, so that was something I wouldn't allow myself to say out loud today, and now I can probably say it out loud," Simpson said. "That was a big thing for me, not repeating the misfortune of four years ago. I didn't want to cry every day until Tokyo 2020."

Simpson said she relied on a special source of motivation throughout the competition: her sister.

Earlier that morning, Simpson read an inspirational note from her little sister, Emily Bradshaw, a U.S. Army fire chief at Fort Stewart, Georgia.

"There was something she wanted me to remember for every step of the way," the Iowa native told the *Des Moines Register*. "The letter she wrote for me to read this morning was, 'You've already climbed Mount Everest. Now, remember to take the time to enjoy the view.'

"I have a mantra I talk about a lot, about being brave. She said to 'be brave is to move forward,' so that was kind of my thought tonight, that today was all about moving forward…Everything in my mind I pointed toward that one goal to keep moving forward."[1]

The joy of the moment was palpable. Simpson grew up riding horses and dreaming of an Olympic equestrian medal, and then a PE teacher suggested she join a cross-country team to make friends. She celebrated the bronze in 2014 with a victory lap.

"I don't even know if you're supposed to run all the way around [the track], but my little sister told me to enjoy the view," she told the assembled press. "I kept thinking of that the whole way. I thought, take your time, enjoy it, you're not guaranteed to get these moments. So I just really wanted to go around and see every person with an American flag and thank them for being here."

What made the win sweeter for Simpson is that she has performed clean in an event known to be affected by performance-enhancing drugs.

"I think you know a tree by the fruit that it bears," Simpson said. "And if a tree bears sour fruit, then the fruit around it are likely infected. I live my life that way in every way, not just through doping."

The feat was the culmination of Simpson's rapid rise to becoming an elite international-caliber runner. In her sophomore year in college at the University of Colorado, Simpson won her first USA Outdoor title in the steeplechase and went on to compete at the World Championships. As a junior, she qualified for the first ever Olympic women's steeplechase, where she finished ninth and set the American record.

She then made two shifts: She became a professional, and she began running middle-distance races.

In 2011 she came back from injuries to win the 1,500 meters at the World Outdoor Championships, showing the running community she had arrived. She followed that with a win in the 5,000 meters at the USA Outdoor Championships.

In all, Simpson has been a member of three U.S. Olympic teams: in 2008 in the steeplechase and in 2012 and 2016 at 1,500 meters. She remains the second-fastest steeplechaser in U.S. history, and she ranks third on the all-time U.S. list at 1,500 meters and second at 3,000 meters. She is also the U.S. indoor record holder at 2 miles.

Simpson is known not only for her supreme talent and for running clean, but she is also regarded as one of the most mentally tough competitors in her sport. That, her positive outlook on life, and her faith serve as the three pillars of her approach to running and to life.

"My sport is a very public thing, and I feel like the most vulnerable place for me is on the starting line of a race," she said. "You're out there, everyone's watching, and you have a lot to prove in that moment—and the race hasn't quite started yet.

"In contrast to that, I feel like my faith is something that is so individual, it's never measured against another human being. It's where I don't feel vulnerable. It's where a lot of my self-worth and a lot of my understanding of what is important to me, what I want to achieve in life, comes from."

All of this has carried Simpson through her disappointments on the track, such as the 2015 World Championships in Beijing, where she was cruising along with two laps to go before she kicked off one of her shoes. She kept running and finished eleventh, walking away with a bloodied foot.

"You can't run on a foot that doesn't have skin," she said after the race.

Ever the competitor, she would have done so if she could. Still, she remains balanced, knowing that her ultimate value is not found in her results.

"I really feel like my faith is often what props up my running, instead of the other way around," Simpson said. "You can win the world championships and then still place last in the 800 meters. There's not nearly as much consistency to rely on in an athletic career as there is in a faith.

"I know this world is so fickle. It gives so much, but it takes so much. And so I think the older I get and the more I experience, I realize you really can't rely on anything in this world to be a stable foundation.

"In my life, Christ is the most amazing constant because He's always the same, He's never going anywhere, and the value I have—when I see my life through His eyes and see the value that He gives me—doesn't change. Whether I'm a great athlete or whether I decide to retire and become a mom or if I want to have a different career, my value doesn't change."

"You can only govern men by serving them."

—VICTOR COUSIN

character
sway guidance
influence management

LEADERSHIP

authority power
pilotage clout
initiative direction
capacity impact

KELLY CLARK

In 1955 James Dean starred in the groundbreaking film *Rebel Without a Cause*, depicting the moral decay of America's confused suburban middle-class youth.

Were a film to be produced today on the life of champion snowboarder Kelly Clark, the title might be *Rebel with a Cause*.

In many ways, Clark is the antithesis of the snowboarding culture. Marching to the beat of her own drum? Check. Coloring outside the lines? You bet. Following her heart rather than the rules. Absolutely. Rebel? Oh, yeah.

Yet to see how Clark is different, all one must do is look at her board. Rather than being plastered with stickers of her sponsors in the most prominent positions, Clark's board has "Jesus—I cannot hide my love" in large script letters front and center.

Like most of the snowboarding culture, most of Clark's personality is always front and center.

Snowboarding is known for baggy pants, tattoos, nose rings, Monster drinks, hard rock music blasting at concert-level decibels, and fearless athletes who comprise the winter version of the '80's SoCal surf culture. It's a mix of sport, personal expression, and Lollapalooza.

So imagine how Clark stands out when, after finishing out of the medals in a competition, she tells the waiting press corps, "I love Jesus. It's more joyful knowing Him than all that snowboarding stuff. And so being able to snowboard for Him is amazing. I love Jesus, and I guess everyone can tell."

Yes, they can.

Eschewing the typical hard rock or metal music choices to accompany her runs, Clark has been known to use "O Praise Him" from Christian worship artist David Crowder instead. But expressing her faith in an atmosphere like the X Games, where sponsorship is king, is the ultimate rebel move. One of the world's top snowboarders is constantly taking a risk in a world where faith is not a popular topic of conversation. Rebels, however, go where nobody else dares go.

Her faith, packed inside an X Games persona, is what makes Clark the ultimate dichotomy.

Clark is the winningest performer in half-pipe history, male or female, with more than 70 wins in competition. She stood on 23 podiums before she was a legal adult. Since then, she's added over ten X Games medals, nine of them gold. She is a four-time Winter Olympian, winning gold in the half-pipe at the 2002 Winter Olympics in Salt Lake City and then bronze in both 2010 and 2014.

Clark thought this success would fulfill her. Instead, it exacerbated her emptiness.

"I was lonely and depressed," she said. "I wanted to die."

She was 18 and found herself at a place where she had accomplished everything she had set out to do. What does one do when they achieve all their goals before they hit 20?

"I had money. I had fame. I had an Olympic gold medal. I had won every major snowboarding event I had ever dreamed of winning when I was a kid," she said. "And I had poured everything I have into snowboarding.

"Apart from that, I didn't have a whole lot going on in my life. I didn't really know who I was and what I was doing. Everyone knew me as Kelly Clark—pro snowboarder Kelly Clark—Olympic gold medalist, and that's who I was. That's who I was to other people, and that's who I was to myself. I was thinking, *If this is what life is, if I've accomplished it all, if this is everything, then I don't want to do it anymore."*

A chance encounter at a tournament changed that. Clark overheard other competitors talking about God.

"I was doing well in the contest, and I qualified for the finals that afternoon," she recalls. "But at the bottom of the pipe this girl had come down and she had fallen on both runs and was crying. I was half paying attention to her conversation, and her friend was trying to make her laugh and said, 'Hey, it's all right. God still loves you.' There was something about that comment that caught my attention that I couldn't shake.

"They said God loved everyone," she continued. "But I wondered if He could really love me."

Later that night, desperate and depressed, Kelly decided to pick up the Bible in her hotel room. She had a hard time understanding what she read.

"As I started looking at the Bible, I realized I didn't know where to look or where to start," she said. "There is something getting stirred up inside of me, and I don't know what to do."

Nearly desperate at this point, Clark found someone who could explain it to her.

"I found out that the girl who made the comment [at the bottom of the pipe] was staying in my hotel," she said. "I knocked on her door and said, 'Hey, my name's Kelly, and I think you might be a Christian, and I think you need to tell me about God.'"

That moment began a change in thinking for Clark.

"I spent the next four months thinking, *Okay, God, if You're real, reveal Yourself to me,"* she said. "I got to the end of my season, and I asked myself a few questions, like, 'Could I ever wake up another day and not think about God?' And the answer was no, because I was thinking about Him every day, and He was real and in my life.

"That was a huge shifting point for me where my snowboarding became this amazing expression and fun thing rather than this thing I had to do. It became this thing I was made to do and I could actually enjoy. And there was so much freedom in it because I wasn't doing it to prove to people who I was.

"Through my relationship with God, I learned who I was and was comfortable in who I was. But I'll tell you, I've never had more fun snow-boarding, and I've never been freer."

Spoken like a true rebel.

Since then she has attacked every competition with a fervor, typically flying higher than her competitors, hitting 900-degree spins, and most of the time sticking landings. For Clark, every competition is a leap of faith. And while not every leap results in a medal, she is undaunted.

"No regrets," Clark said. "I put it all on the line. It's just who I am. Playing it safe is always a risk. It comes with the risk of regret."

Her fearlessness—performing some of the most radical flips and tricks that made her a pioneer in the sport—continues to keep her driven to attempt new and more radical moves.

One of the bold moves she made off the slopes was to launch the Kelly Clark Foundation in 2010, which empowers youth by using snowboard-ing as the medium for success. She is committed to making snowboard-ing more financially accessible to all people, increasing and diversifying participation in the snowboard industry, and facilitating opportunities for the widespread use of snowboarding as a tool for personal success. The foundation has awarded more than $100,000 to promising young snow-boarders to overcome financial barriers and allow them to pursue their dreams.

Through it all, she continues to live out her dreams.

"God is blessing me so much by allowing me to do what I love to do."

CASE KEENUM

»FACTOIDS

He married his high school sweetheart, Kimberly.

Case's mom was his wife's fifth-grade PE teacher.

That Case Keenum led the Minnesota Vikings to the brink of a berth in Super Bowl LII was a surprise to nearly everyone.

Everyone, that is, except those with the last name of Keenum.

Keenum's family has watched him prove doubters wrong throughout his football career.

As a high school quarterback in Abilene, Texas, he threw for 48 touchdowns, ran for another 41 in 42 games, and led Wylie High to the state championship. Yet college recruiters stayed away. Keenum was ranked as the 1,818th recruit in the nation by 247Sports. His numbers created some interest, but when coaches came down and saw his slight stature and less than ideal arm strength, they backed away.

His only scholarship offer came from the University of Houston. There, Keenum finished his career by throwing for more yards and more touchdowns than any quarterback in Division I history. Over his four years, he threw for more than 19,000 yards and 155 touchdowns. His statistics in three of his last four seasons as a Cougar are video game-like: more than 5,000 yards passing each year with 44, 44, and 48 touchdowns.

Even after his record-breaking college career, Keenum did not hear his name called at the 2012 NFL draft. Imagine, the player who threw for more yards and more touchdowns in the history of the game, and no one was interested. But at just a hair over six feet tall, Keenum is not the ideal NFL quarterback specimen. Only one team—the Houston Texans—even offered him a free agent opportunity. He took it.

The Texans released him before the season started and then re-signed him to the practice squad. What followed was a bit of a roller-coaster existence. Keenum was cut by the Texans just before the start of the 2014 season and picked up by the St. Louis Rams. The Rams waived him two months later but signed him to their practice squad. Before the season was over, he was re-signed by the Texans for a second stint.

The Rams reacquired him in 2015—trading a seventh-round draft pick for him—and Keenum stayed with the team for two seasons, becoming their starter for most of the 2016 season. The Rams chose not to re-sign him for the 2017 season when his contract expired, and Keenum was a free agent. Over five seasons in the league, Keenum had collected 24 starts and performed admirably, yet now he was once again looking for a new home.

The Chicago Bears and Buffalo Bills both expressed interest, but only the Vikings indicated they really wanted him.

Minnesota was looking for some insurance. Teddy Bridgewater, the 2015 starting quarterback, had suffered a horrendous knee injury, and his return was uncertain. His replacement, Sam Bradford, had a history of injuries and a balky knee. Keenum was brought in as a safeguard and offered a one-year contract.

Throughout the 2017 preseason, Keenum was running neck-and-neck with Taylor Heinicke to make the roster. As the regular season drew near, Keenum began to look more comfortable in the Vikings offense and ended up winning the backup job.

After winning their season opener under Bradford, who was subsequently named the NFC Offensive Player of the Week, the Vikings played at Pittsburgh in week two. Bradford's knee was giving him trouble, and when game time hit, he was unable to play. On Minnesota's first possession, Keenum ran out to the huddle.

"Don't worry about this," he told his teammates. "I've got it. Now, let's roll."

Keenum struggled through a loss to the Steelers, but his leadership had an impact on his teammates. They were ready to follow him.

He ended up leading them to 11 wins in 14 games. He had the second-best completion percentage in the league at 67.6% and the NFL's seventh-highest passer rating at 98.3. He passed for 3,547 yards and 22 touchdowns with just 7 interceptions and was a contender for the league's MVP Award.

"I've had a chip on my shoulder for a long time," Keenum told Bleacher Report. "It's driven me to work hard my whole career. I am who I am. I don't apologize about it. I don't worry about it.

"My whole life, I've been the underdog. I've been reminding myself a lot that I can do it, and I know this team has my back…There are a lot of people's opinions that don't matter."[1]

He played through the 2017 season without any real security. He had just a one-year deal, and he knew either Bradford or Bridgewater—or both—could come back at any time and take his job. Was he simply a caretaker or was he in the right place at the right time to truly come into his own?

His leadership was undoubtedly a key to the Vikings making it to the 2017 NFC Championship game in what was one of the most dramatic finishes in league history. The Vikings trailed the New Orleans Saints 24-23 with ten seconds left in the game, and in the huddle Keenum called a play the team refers to as "Seven Heaven." Keenum dropped back and found receiver Stefon Diggs 20 yards downfield and near the sideline. After a missed tackle, Diggs sprinted into the end zone with a 61-yard walk-off touchdown pass called "the Minnesota Miracle." Just like that, the Vikings were headed to the title game.

On the field after the game, Keenum told the nation, the win "will probably go down as the third-best moment of my life, after giving my life to Jesus Christ and marrying my wife."

"Being a kid growing up, that's what you do in the backyard," he later told the assembled press. "Thirty seconds to go, down by two, fourth quarter of the playoffs. That's what you dream about."

The play will long be remembered for its drama, but it will also be the play that finally brought credibility to Keenum, whose NFL dreams have come true.

Keenum's performance was a testament to the work he put in. He threw himself into studying the Vikings playbook and watched thousands of hours of film. He also used Virtual Reality to indoctrinate himself into the team's offense. According to the Vikings, Keenum took more than 2,600 VR play reps so he could mentally run through every one of the Vikings plays off the field and visualize them in real time. The result was Keenum got better as the season went on, and he became more comfortable with the offense. The prep paid off. For the 2017 season, his QBR under pressure rating was the best in the NFL.

"I've never seen anyone prepare the way he does," Vikings receiver Adam Thielen told Bleacher Report. "He's always coming to us with things he sees on tape or things he can do a little better job of. And talking about how we can attack defenses. I think he takes it to another level."[2]

During the 2017 season, when Thielen arrived at the Vikings facility at 6:30 each morning, he found Keenum had already been there for an hour, watching tape and taking notes. After the Vikings offense completed practice and meetings on Wednesdays and Thursdays, Keenum often watched tape for another hour or two with his receivers. He wanted to be as prepared as possible, which is typical of Keenum.

Keenum's dad, Steve, is a former football coach who now works with the Fellowship of Christian Athletes. He compares his son's situation to the biblical story of David.

"God was going to choose a king," Steve told Bleacher Report. "He had Samuel look at all these guys. He saw the Schwarzenegger-type guys, all kinds. God said no to all of them. Finally, he came to this one small guy, David. They said, 'He can't be the one.' Well, they were looking at the wrong stuff. They were looking at the outside. And I think that's what's happened with Case."[3]

What's inside Keenum and oozes out is faith, grit, and confidence.

"I think I can make every throw in the book," he said. "Am I perfect? No. Is anybody?"

"Case is a pretty cool customer," Vikings head coach Mike Zimmer said. "He has a big chip on his shoulder. He's always trying to prove people wrong. I do love that about him."[4]

"The guys who play at a high level probably think they are better than they are, and that's all right," Adam Thielen told NBC Sports. "He definitely has that. He doesn't care what people think. He knows he can play at a high level."[5]

Where does his confidence come from? His father says Case has been good at just about everything he's ever done. In high school, not only did he succeed at quarterback, but he was also all-state basketball. When he played varsity baseball as a freshman, he hit the ball off the outfield wall in each of his first two at-bats. Although he was not the football team's kicker, he convinced his coach to use him for a field-goal attempt on the opening drive of the season, and he drilled a 47-yarder. He's also a scratch golfer and an expert bowhunter.

"I really feel he has the ability to make a play at the most crucial time," said former Vikings offensive coordinator Pat Shurmur. "He's done that for us...He's just a really good player."[6]

And a really good teammate.

"He's a guy you want to play for," Thielen said.

"He's willing to shoulder the blame for things that are not his fault," Vikings guard Joe Berger told Fox Sports. "That's the quality I admire most about him. I got beat for a sack late in the game. Case said he should have got the ball out faster. Clearly, it was the right guard's fault, not his fault."[7]

It was Keenum who was leading the cheers when Bridgewater took his first snaps in a game, 16 months after his injury.

"It was great," Bridgewater told Vikings.com. "It was better seeing Case leading the chant. Case is an awesome guy, and to see him standing behind me was just amazing."[8]

"What I want is to be a great teammate," Keenum said. "I want guys in the locker room to remember the relationships I've had with them. That's important for me, more than any other external goal—to impact guys in the locker room."

He is impacting the locker room, and he is finally recognized as the quarterback of a playoff team.

"He just wanted a chance," his dad said. "He's got to have the knack. It's just a God-given, innate thing he's maximized by working hard."[9]

"I've had people tell me every step of the way that I shouldn't be able to do this, or I can't do this—I'm too short, I'm too slow, too whatever," Keenum said. "I try not to play to prove those people wrong. Instead, I try to play to prove people right who have believed in me—whether it's coaches, family members, friends."[10]

"He's come to the realization like a lot of people in big situations that there are things that are really too big to do by yourself, and in order to stay grounded you have to find somebody or something you believe strongly in," his dad said. "I think his faith has been that for him."[11]

"God has equipped me with exactly what I need, so it's important I do the best I can with what He has given me," Keenum said.

"When nobody is looking, he's the same Case as when everybody is looking at him," Thielen told Bleacher Report. "A lot of people can talk about their faith. When you live it every day and act on the Word of God, it's pretty cool to see. He doesn't just talk; he acts upon it and leads by example. It helps me become a better person of faith."[12]

During the off-season following his impressive run with the Vikings, Keenum signed a multimillion-dollar free agent contract with the Denver Broncos for the 2018 season. He was finally a wanted man.

"You just realize that football is fickle; it's not going to be there all the time," Keenum told the St. Paul *Pioneer Press*. "Just getting my priorities straight and knowing the true reason I play the game are things I take pride in. They are why I do what I do. I'm not playing for the name on the back of my jersey. I'm playing to glorify God. He's given me talents, and I'm trying to maximize those talents however I can."[13]

*"The pessimist complains about the wind.
The optimist expects it to change.
The leader adjusts the sails."*

JOHN MAXWELL

BRAD STEVENS

»FACTOIDS

His wife, Tracy, is an attorney who negotiates his contracts.

At age five, he watched tapes of basketball games before going to afternoon kindergarten.

He has been called a boy genius, a wunderkind, a prodigy. Yet Brad Stevens will have no part of such lionization. He is, after all, just a basketball coach. Albeit coach of the most venerated franchise in NBA history, the Boston Celtics.

How Stevens got here is quite a story. The fact he has heard all about how great he is and has maintained his humility is another story in itself.

In 2000 Stevens left his job at the Eli Lilly Company and took a pay cut to be a volunteer graduate-manager at Butler University. He was promoted to a full-time assistant position for the 2001–02 season, but it took him five years to get back to the salary level of the job he had left at Lilly. Stevens devoured tape and attended coaching retreats. He was in a constant learning mode.

In 2007, after six years as an assistant, the 30-year-old Stevens was selected as Butler's head coach.

In his first year at the helm, Stevens led Butler to 30 wins, making him the third-youngest head coach in NCAA Division I history to do so.

In his third year Stevens broke the NCAA record for most wins in a coach's first three years and took Butler to the first Final Four appearance in school history. His team narrowly lost to Duke 61-59 in the national championship game. When Butler made the Final Four again during the 2011–12 season, Stevens became the youngest coach ever to lead his team to two Final Fours.

"Their defensive schemes were so much more sophisticated than what you see in most of college basketball," Stevens's former college coach Bill Fenlon told *Sports Illustrated*. "It was stunning at times, the way those Butler kids were able to see things before they happened and communicate with each other."[1]

The same was true on offense.

"I don't want to say they were flawless," Cleveland State coach Gary Waters told *SI*, "but Brad's teams were absolutely great in situational execution."[2]

After Stevens compiled a record of 166-49 (a winning percentage of .772) over six seasons and made five NCAA tournament appearances, both college programs and NBA teams were looking his way. Some were comparing him to the legendary John Wooden.

As many as ten major college programs pursued Stevens. Each time he politely declined. He and his wife, Tracy, thought they would never leave Butler for another college job. But the NBA always stuck in the back of Stevens's mind.

He would watch NBA games, not just to see his former players, but also to learn. Tracy often found scraps of paper around the house with plays drawn on them.

"He is a lifelong learner," Tracy told *Sports Illustrated*.[3]

In the summer of 2013, Celtics president Danny Ainge contacted Stevens about the opening in Boston. A month later Ainge stunned many in the basketball world by announcing Stevens's hiring with a six-year, $22-million contract to the 36-year-old college coach.

While some were stunned, it made perfect sense to others. The smart coach with an ever-cool demeanor and high character, who was relational with players, and who was given to intensive study made it work in the NBA and was a great fit in Boston, where the team was in the midst of an overhaul and trying to return to its former pinnacle.

"We hired him because he's a great person," Ainge told *Sports Illustrated*. "He's a hard worker, and he's very smart. It's a good formula for success."[4]

Seventeen NBA championship banners ring the ceiling of the Boston Garden. The first came in 1956–57, the last in 2007–08. The names of hoop legends are visible all over, the ghosts of championships past: Auerbach, Cousy, Russell, Heinsohn, Havlicek, Cowens, McHale, Bird, and more. The winningest franchise in basketball history put its keys in the hands of Stevens.

The coach was tasked with the job of rebuilding a Celtics squad that was a lottery team the year before his hiring. He spent his first two months on the job digging into Celtics history and understanding the mystique. He met and talked with a number of former coaches and players. He wasn't just taking an NBA job, he was taking *the* NBA job.

He instantly established a rapport with his players. His youth helped, as did his keen awareness that it wouldn't work well if he got too close to the players.

The turnaround was stunning. The Celtics lacked star talent when Stevens arrived. He went 25-57 in his first season and then jumped up 15 wins in year two to 40-42 and made the playoffs. In the 2017-18 season, he took the Celtics to within one game of the NBA Finals—without the team's top two players in Kyrie Irving and Gordon Hayward. The meteoric rise took everyone in Boston by surprise except Stevens and Ainge.

"The great challenge of coaching is that team dynamics always make it difficult, no matter what," Stevens said. "You always have a lot going on [around] your team, and you've got to get a group of people to try to play as well as they can together. Every year, that's going to be the greatest challenge.

"We look at guys who might have a chip on their shoulder," he said. "That's been a big deal for us. It's something that can be contagious, but it has to be recruited. At this level you have to draft and sign guys who have that attitude. It's hard to create an environment if those guys didn't bring that with them."

Along with the attitude, Stevens looks to build his team with players who are smart and do the right things.

"You look for high-IQ players, and savvy players…Because it's a long year, you see a lot of situations—you have to change on the fly, you have to tweak on a dime," Stevens said. "To me, all the intangible, subjective things you can't measure are more important than the things you can."

By Stevens's fourth year, things were in high gear. The Celtics were a title contender, going 53-29 and playing in the Eastern Conference finals. In 2017–18, after acquiring Kyrie Irving, Boston was the favorite in the East to advance to the NBA Championship.

How did it happen? Stevens, the lifelong learner, quickly became one of the strongest in-game strategy coaches in the NBA. He mixes and matches different lineups when situations call for a different approach. Players are comfortable with the changes because of the level of trust he has engendered with them.

"Every NBA player has an elite strength," Stevens told *Sports Illustrated*. "Some of them have ten of 'em, and those guys are the very best in the league, right? But every one of 'em is here for a reason. And there are times when you can really soar with that skill, and there are times when they may not be as effective."[5]

Stevens has a unique feel for when those times are coming before they happen. This knack is one of the reasons his teams have been so successful: His decisions make good players look even better.

"He brings the ultimate unwavering confidence. So chill, but assertive, demanding. He does it in just the most unique way," Irving said on J.J. Redick's podcast. "And it's like almost bringing college to the NBA. I feel that we're a very professional team, but the way we run things and the way we demand excellence out of each other is something like being on a college team. Just our film study, our preparation, our walk throughs, our shootarounds.

"He has adjusted to the NBA life, but yet he still remains and has the high-character integrity of being the up-and-coming college coach he was. And he was great in college and then made the transition into the league. He didn't necessarily have the best of teams, but he demanded excellence out of them, and he was always unwavering, he was always chill. And he demands it out of you. I keep saying demands, but…you want to play for him, you want to do it."[6]

"Leading by example," Celtics guard Avery Bradley told Basketball Insiders when asked about Stevens's greatest strength in the locker room. "A lot of the things he does, I think [they] rub off on us. Him preparing for each game—we see how hard he works, and it makes us want to go out there and not only be prepared for him, but be prepared for the team…At the end of the day we're all a team, including the coaches. I respect that."

"Brad and I share a lot of the same values," said Ainge. "Though he is young, I see Brad as a great leader who leads with impeccable character and a strong work ethic. His teams always play hard and execute on both ends of the court. Brad is a coach who has already enjoyed lots of success, and I look forward to working with him towards banner 18."

"He never tries to be somebody else," said former Chicago Bulls coach Tom Thibodeau. "He's humble, he's trustworthy, he's reliable, and he's sincere. The players in the NBA read that, and if they see that he's knowledgeable, they're gonna buy into it."[7]

Ronald Nored, who played for Stevens at Butler and is now a coach in the NBA G League, said of his mentor, "I think he is the most genuine person I have ever met in my life—ever."[8]

"He has found himself to be a public figure, and when he thought about going into coaching, that was not on his radar," Tracy said. "It's hard to balance your public persona and your private persona. He lives with it, and he acts out his faith every day, but he is very private."[9]

"I hope it affects everything I do," Stevens told *Sports Spectrum* of his faith. "Just as I ask our team to try constantly to improve every day, I'm trying to improve every day. And that being the most important aspect of my life, that's the part where I think I've got the greatest room for improvement. I'm really blessed to have not only this great opportunity here, but a great family.

"I'm not a person that gets too wrapped up around one game or one loss. You have to try your best to focus on the next task and try to do as well as you possibly can. It allows me to understand that there is a bigger picture in all of this…because that is not how I get my validation. The verse that always come to my mind is Proverbs 3:5-6: 'Trust in the Lord…In all of your ways and seek him first.' That's what I want to do as a coach."[10]

When asked by the press what his life would be like if he had never left that job at Eli Lilly and taken up coaching, Stevens replied, "If everything else remained the same, I would have been as happy as heck…Friends and family and faith. They're going to take the cake over all this stuff."

"Leadership is tied to conviction. Leaders have a vision of a better future; they feel strongly about the need to go there."

DELORESE AMBROSE

DABO SWINNEY

From the outside, Dabo Swinney may be just about as unlikely a success story as you'll find. He says he didn't even know his own name until the second or third grade.

Yet once you learn what's inside, it is easy to see why Swinney has become one of the winningest coaches in college football and a man top recruits want to play for.

William Christopher "Dabo" Swinney is the head coach of the Clemson Tigers, one of the most successful college football programs of the last decade.

Under Swinney, Clemson is 101-30 over ten years and has played in a bowl game at the end of each season. They won the national championship in 2016 in a thrilling last-second victory over Alabama and have won six other bowl or playoff games.

Swinney was selected as the Bear Bryant Coach of the Year in both 2015 and 2016. In 2015 the Associated Press, ESPN, the Sporting News, the Walter Camp Foundation, and the American Football Coaches Association all named him national coach of the year.

As good as these accomplishments have been on the field, Swinney's teams may have been more impressive in the classroom. Over a six-year period, through 2017, his teams finished among the nation's top ten in the NCAA's Academic Progress Report. Since 2009, 157 of his 162 seniors have earned their degree at Clemson. Four of the other five are playing in the NFL.

How did this man from such an unlikely beginning become so proficient in delivering results?

"I have an MBA," Swinney told ESPN, "but my PhD is in people. Everything I do is about relationships."[1]

Relationships are at the very center of what Swinney is all about because of the relationships that affected him during his childhood. Those relationships also inspired him.

His mother, Carol McIntosh, contracted polio when she was two years old. She spent years in the hospital, finally walking out after a decade of treatment and surgeries and doctors telling her she would never walk again.

Dabo's father, Ervil Swinney, married Carol two weeks after she graduated high school. When Dabo was born, his older brother struggled to say "that boy" when referring to Dabo. "That boy" came out "Dabo" and the name stuck.

If Dabo's father passed on one thing to him as a child, it was a love for Alabama football. The two spent hours watching anything related to the Crimson Tide.

"My dad was the biggest Alabama fan ever, and I was brainwashed," Swinney told ESPN. "In Alabama, when you come out of the hospital, they have to stamp your birth certificate with either Alabama or Auburn or you don't leave.

"That's all I knew. I always told people Alabama was the smartest state because it has four A's and a B."[2]

Dabo's dream was to play football at Alabama for the legendary Paul "Bear" Bryant. But before he could get there, the Swinney family hit hard times. Swinney's brother was seriously injured in a car accident. He lost his memory and battled alcohol addiction and depression for years. Then financial issues led Ervil to drink. When he drank, he often became violent.

Swinney's parents divorced, and Dabo and his mom moved frequently, sometimes staying at motels while Carol earned eight dollars an hour working at a department store. Through it all, Dabo became an honor roll student and enrolled at Alabama.

After settling in on the Tuscaloosa campus, Dabo invited Carol to live with him. He and his mom shared a room, and his roommate took the other room. The arrangement worked for three years, and then mother and son moved into a three-bedroom home.

"It was hard, and our hearts were so broken," Carol said. "But those were some of the happiest times of my life because we were together, we were safe, and we were peaceful. We didn't have much, but we had everything we needed…We were together."[3]

"You just do what you have to do, but I loved having my mom there," Swinney said. "It was a little different at first, but when you're in the middle of situations in your life, you just make the best of it. That's kind of how I've always lived my life. That's to me what true peace and happiness are all about."

Swinney was a walk-on receiver at Alabama, and coach Gene Stallings gave him a scholarship in 1991. Dabo concluded his career as a starter in the Tide's national championship victory over Miami in the 1993 Orange Bowl.

"He was an average player," Stallings told ESPN. "He wanted to be a great player, but he just wasn't blessed with a lot of talent. He had a lot of heart. I knew he was extremely poor, and I gave him a scholarship. I'm glad I did because he needed one."[4]

Shortly after the championship win, Swinney reconciled with Ervil, who was starting to get his life back together.

"He quit drinking. He quit smoking. He got his life right with the Lord, and it was amazing to watch the last 14 or 15 years of his life. He figured it all out, and it was special," Swinney said.

In 1993 Stallings hired Swinney as a graduate assistant and then promoted him to a full-time assistant three years later. In 2003 Swinney joined the staff at Clemson, and midway through the 2008 season he was promoted to interim head coach and then made the full-time coach at the end of that season. Since then, he and the Tigers have been on a roll.

In 2016, while Swinney was leading Clemson to the national championship, he learned Ervil was battling cancer and invited him to live with him. The days before his father's death were some of the sweetest Swinney ever shared with him. Swinney still has four voicemails from his father on his cellphone and listens to them often.

Relationship rivers run deep in Dabo. It is why he has made it his mission to make Clemson more than just a football program. He wants it to be family.

"Football is just what we do. It's not really who we are," defensive coordinator Brent Venables said. "He creates an incredible culture that builds up instead of tears down young people. He keeps the main things the main things. He lets us enjoy our life as husbands and fathers, and he does a super job of making sure our players have a great college experience."[5]

"We believe in his vision, and we believe in who he is as a person," co-offensive coordinator Tony Elliott agreed.[6]

"Nick Saban has his process," Thad Turnipseed, Clemson's director of recruiting and external affairs and a former Saban associate told ESPN of the Alabama coach. "Dabo built a culture."[7]

To keep that culture and family atmosphere, Swinney designed Clemson's $55 million football facility, which was completed in 2017. The building includes a two-story chute slide, a golf simulator, and a Wiffle ball field. Swinney added these to remind his players to have fun, that they are a family. For the fun elements, players can practice their golf swing, work on their résumé, get involved in charity work, have a personally customized meal, or simply grab a nap.

"Football, to me, is just the unique opportunity to have a pathway into their lives," Swinney told ESPN. "I want them to truly love their experience and not just be a football player, but to grow and be a person of excellence that just happens to be a good football player too. And my philosophy is: If we develop them that way, football will take care of itself because they create habits of excellence that carry over."[8]

Again, for Swinney, it is all about relationship. For most of the players, Swinney is like their dad.

"Anybody can get up there and tell them what to do," Swinney said. "If you can't articulate why you need to do it, they won't listen. It's a different world. If my coach told me to go run them bleachers, you didn't ask questions. I turned around and started running until he said stop. Now they'll still run bleachers, but you better be able to tell them why."

Each year Swinney develops a notebook that serves as an operational Bible of sorts for the coming season. It's not just x's and o's.

"Probably a third of this book is about building men, about character," Turnipseed told ESPN.[9]

Swinney's notebook is filled with motivational sayings: Iron sharpens iron. Serve a player's heart, not his talent. How you do something is how you do everything. The little things lead to big things.

He's also placed these hallmark axioms on the walls of the football building. He and his staff repeat them again and again throughout the season.

"You have to be intentional," Swinney said. "I'm very focused on the culture we have and on nurturing that. Whether it's how we discipline, how we recruit, how we staff, how we respond to something great, something bad. It's all of those things."

His relational heart is genuine and extends beyond his players. It was on display in an unusual way during the 2017 season, in the aftermath of a devastating upset loss to Syracuse. Swinney went to the Orange locker room to applaud the players who had just beat him.

"He came in and congratulated us, just saying, 'Great win,' and that was probably one of the most class-act things I've ever seen," Syracuse linebacker Zaire Franklin said. "I've never heard of a coach doing that before. I have a lot of respect for that."[10]

"I think we'll look back in 25 years," Turnipseed said, "and he will have changed college football."[11]

Although he has been very good at it, Swinney's desire goes beyond winning. He is focused on impacting the student-athletes who play for him and giving them the father figure he missed out on for several years.

"The one thing I will say about Coach Swinney is that he genuinely cares about people," Tigers receiver Hunter Renfrow told *Sports Spectrum*. "He's such a great role model for anyone. Whether you're a receiver or an offensive lineman, whoever it is. He's taught me far more about life then he has football. And that's a credit to him and what he believes in."[12]

"I just try to be who I am and I try to be transparent. I don't try to judge people or anything like that," Swinney said in a video interview with the Associated Press. "I just try to live my life in a way that I hope is pleasing to my Maker, but as far as our program, we just try to challenge these guys to be the best that they can be each and every day…I hope that regardless of what somebody's faith is, I hope that whether they choose the faith that I have or not, I hope that I can be a good example for them in life, as far as being a good husband and good father."

"Most of the important things in the world have been accomplished by people who kept on trying when there seemed to be no hope at all."

—DALE CARNEGIE

steadfastness
resolve persistence
determination

PERSEVERANCE

purposefulness
drive strength of purpose
spunk firmness
backbone endurance
dedication

SIMONE BILES

> **»FACTOIDS**

She is afraid of bees.

She has four German shepherds at home: Maggie, Atlas, Lily, and Bella.

Some would say the greatest athlete in America stands less than five feet tall.

Many have called her the GOAT (greatest of all time).

No argument here.

Simone Biles—all four-feet-nine of her—wowed the world at the 2016 Summer Olympic Games in Rio de Janeiro. Biles staked her claim as the greatest female gymnast ever with a scintillating performance in which she exhibited far-reaching excellence.

She won five medals at the games, four of them gold. She won the all-around championship by an astounding two full points in a sport in which champions are decided by tenths and even hundredths of a point. She also took gold in the floor exercise and the vault, and she led the team to gold in the overall team competition. She added a bronze in the balance beam. With her three straight world championship golds (2013, 2014, and 2015) coming into the games, she became the first gymnast ever to sweep all the major all-around titles in an Olympic four-year period.

It was a performance that left fans, teammates, opponents, and admirers in awe.

"She's definitely the best female gymnast there's ever been," said Canada's Ellie Black, who finished fifth in the all-around. "I don't think she's human."[1]

"Nobody else in the world can do her floor routine," said Isabela Onyshko, another Canuck.[2]

"It just shows how amazing she is and how mentally tough she is," said U.S. teammate Aly Raisman, who won two medals herself. "I don't even consider myself competing against her. It's like she's at another level. She's incredible…I'm in awe watching her, and I train with her every day."[3]

"She may be the most talented gymnast I've ever seen in my life, honestly," said 1984 gold medal gymnast Mary Lou Retton. "And I don't even think she's tapped into what she really can do. I think she's unbeatable."[4]

"She's the best gymnast that's ever lived on the women's side for sure," agreed Nastia Liukin, the 2008 Olympic all-around champion. "She's the most talented gymnast I've ever seen in my life, and obviously the Olympics will seal the deal. But even with 14 world championship medals, she's the best!"[5]

While Biles was understandably excited about her performance, she insists the most exciting part of the Olympic experience for her was winning the team gold with her teammates—the group who gained the moniker the "Final Five" before the games began.

"To be part of the Final Five was really amazing," Biles told the international press corps in the aftermath of her gold haul. "It's something I'll cherish in my heart forever. And it's something we'll always be connected with because we did so well at the games. And the bond we've had—we're like sisters. We're really good friends, and we want the best for each other. The success we brought back to the States and shared with them was something unbelievable."

What makes all this more unbelievable is Biles's backstory, the kind Hollywood producers make movies about.

"My journey to the 2016 Olympics started on a daycare field trip," Biles shared on her website. "You might think that going from a girl in foster care to being an Olympic gold medalist in Rio de Janeiro is the most amazing part of my journey. It isn't. It's how I got there—or more accurately, who got me there—that is most miraculous…How my faith and my family made my wildest dreams come true."[6]

Biles was born in Ohio, the daughter of a fatherless home. She was shuffled between a drug-addicted mother and foster homes.

"My biological mom was suffering with drugs and alcohol," Biles said. "So [my sister and I] were taken into foster care. And we were in foster care for a little bit until my grandparents decided to take us in."

Biles's maternal grandparents, Ron and Nellie Biles, adopted her and her sister, Adria, when they were six and four respectively. They moved her to a suburb of Houston, Texas. Ron was an air force veteran and a retired air traffic controller; Nellie was a retired nurse. They provided the girls with love and stability.

"It was meant to be. I mean, without a shadow of a doubt nothing was supposed to be different, and it's the best decision we've ever made," Nellie said of the adoption.

Ron and Nellie were called Grandpa and Grandma by Simone and Adria when they first moved in. That changed one day when Nellie told the girls, "It's up to you guys. If you want to, you can call us Mom and Dad."

"I went upstairs," Biles told *Texas Monthly*, "and tried practicing it in the mirror—'Mom, Dad, Mom, Dad.' Then I went downstairs, and she [Nellie] was in the kitchen. I looked up at her, and I was like, 'Mom?' She said, 'Yes!'"[7]

Mom and Dad provided a secure environment in which they instilled values. They also encouraged Simone to put her life in God's hands.

"I am a very prayerful person, so I encourage my children to do the same thing too, to pray," Nellie said. "And I know it doesn't matter what situation you are ever in. You just put it in the hands of the Lord, and He's going to walk you through it."[8]

"I was taught that you can go to Him for anything, and He's the One who directs your life," Biles added, reflecting on Nellie's influence. "She would always tell you if you don't know, leave it up to God. Pray to Him about it."

It was in that environment that Biles first displayed a prowess for flying and flipping.

"She'd want me to catch her when she bounced off things," her adopted brother Ron Jr. told *Sports Illustrated*. "She used to use my arm for pull-ups. She'd be smiling and laughing. If I stopped, she'd make me straighten it and hold it for her again. I said, 'Simone, that's not normal.'"[9]

Simone's interest in gymnastics was piqued at age six when she took a daycare field trip to Bannon's Gymnastix. Aimee Boorman, Biles's coach during her incredible championship run, was a coach at Bannon's at the time. After Simone's first few visits to the gym, Boorman recognized her talent and sent a letter to Ron and Nellie, asking them to enroll her in a class.

"She had better balance on her hands than the other girls had on their feet," Boorman, who was Biles's coach for 11 years, recalled to *Sports Illustrated*. "She'd have a conversation and hold a handstand at the same time."[10]

Simone's parents had told her she should always stay grounded but always reach for the sky. Plus they weren't sure if it was such a good idea for Biles to keep doing backflips off their mailbox. So off she went to Bannon's to see just how high she could fly. Turns out it was much higher than just about anyone—ever.

Biles won a gold medal in the floor exercise and a bronze in vault at the 2010 Women's Junior Olympic National Championships. Less than two years later she was dominating the sport.

In her first year as a senior competitor in 2013, Biles announced her presence at her first world championship. She won the all-around title (the first African American to do so), won gold in the floor exercise, a silver in vault, and a bronze in balance beam.

"One of my proudest moments was probably the 2013 World's," Biles said, "because I proved to myself that I could do things that I didn't think I could. I guess I didn't really believe everyone when they told me how good I was, and so for me to go out there and [win], I kind of started to believe it…I proved to myself that I do have the confidence to go out there and hit it like I do in practice."

At the 2014 World Championships, she won four golds: the women's team competition, the individual all-around, balance beam, and floor exercise events. She also took silver in vault.

Simone made it three for three in 2015, winning the all-around, as well as the balance beam and floor exercise titles, and bringing home a bronze in vault and a gold in the team title. With 14 total world championship medals, she has the most ever laurels earned by a U.S. gymnast, male or female. Her ten world championship gold medals are the most won by a female gymnast in the sport's history.

"I think the proudest moment I had of Simone's life is her talking to me and telling me she wants to go an elite track of gymnastics to compete for her country," Nellie told CBN News. "A little girl told me that, and she did it."

She did, but she would have to wait. Biles was too young to qualify for the 2012 London Olympics. So she spent four more years pursuing her dream and waiting for Rio to make an even greater mark on the sport.

"I guess I loved the freedom of the sport. There was no right or wrong that you could do. You didn't have to have one particular body type," she said. "You made everything mold into what you were born with.

"I think God gives every individual something special, and mine was talent…My dad always told me not to waste the gift that God's given me because it's a once-in-a-lifetime opportunity. One day I'll be too old to do gymnastics. So for now I have to use it to the best of my ability."

And that she does. Her combination of supreme athleticism, animated personality, and fearless willingness to take risks have set her apart from the rest of the competition and from those who went before her in the sport. She has 19 medals—14 of them gold—to prove it.

"I think what sets me apart is how bubbly [I am] and how much joy I find in [the sport], because it really does come all from inside whenever I go out there on the floor," Biles said. "Everyone is so serious out there, and I'm like, 'Hey, guys!'…That's how I have fun doing what I do, and it's how it works best for me and how I get my success out there."

After taking off from training in 2017, Biles was back in the gym in 2018 with her sights on the 2020 Tokyo Olympics.

"That's the ultimate long-term goal," she said of the Tokyo games. "But I try not to think too far ahead of myself."

Biles will be 23 when the Tokyo games begin, and that's ancient by elite women's gymnastics standards.

"You're so young when you think of all these dreams, but once you put hard work and dedication into them, you can really achieve anything," she said. "I think the mind is one of the strongest things you have. I hope, before I end my career, I give all of my energy and effort and my talent toward the sport before I finally like hang up my grips and say I'm done.

"I always say my biggest competitor is myself, because whenever I step out there on the mat, I'm competing against myself to prove I can do this and that I am very well trained and prepared for it. So I always just listen to [my mom's advice] and be the best Simone I can be. It just really sticks with me whenever I go out to competition."

In 2018 Biles painfully acknowledged publicly that she was one of the more than 150 athletes who were sexually abused by former USA Gymnastics team doctor Larry Nassar.

In a statement on her Twitter account, Biles wrote, "I know that this horrific experience *does not* define me. I am much more than this. I am unique, smart, talented, motivated, and passionate. I have promised myself that my story will be much greater than this, and I promise all of you that I will never give up. I love this sport too much, and I have never been a quitter. I won't let one man, and the others that enabled him, to steal my love and joy."

Biles shared her inspirational story in her book *Courage to Soar*, released in 2016. She hopes her story will inspire others to persevere through challenges and pursue their dreams.

"I want people to reach for their dreams. If you're willing to put in a lot of work, and if you're focused and determined, you can go really far," Biles told the *Christian Post*. "There are so many people who have inspired me with their love and encouragement along the way—and I want to pass on that inspiration to readers."[11]

"Fall seven times, get up eight."

JAPANESE PROVERB

ABBEY D'AGOSTINO

> **»FACTOIDS**

She was awarded the Pierre de Coubertin Award for her sportsman spirit at the Rio Olympics (1 of only 17 ever so recognized).

She ran her first road race, a 5K, in 2017.

Abbey D'Agostino's run at the 2016 Rio Olympics was one of the greatest moments in the history of sport.

Not because she won.

Not because she finished the race.

But because, unlike most athletes in the history of the Olympics, she put her competitor first. By doing so, she became a shining example of sportsmanship and reflected the Olympic spirit.

The games of the Thirty-First Olympiad in Rio de Janeiro provided thrilling competition. Michael Phelps owned the swimming venue (again). Two Simones took center stage and gold medals: Biles in gymnastics and Manuel shattered a barrier in the pool. U.S. women swept the 110-meter hurdles. And there were so many more memorable moments.

Yet, undoubtedly, the finest moment of the games belonged to Abbey D'Agostino, and it had nothing to do with medals and everything to do with mettle.

At the preliminary heat of the 5,000 meters, Abbey ran for a spot in the finals. The seven-time NCAA champion at Dartmouth College appeared to be one of the best hopes for the United States in the race. She started strong and then disaster hit.

With four and a half laps left in the race, New Zealand's Nikki Hamblin, running in front of Abbey, stumbled and fell. Abbey tripped over Hamblin and also fell. She scrambled to her feet, but Hamblin remained on the ground. Abbey could have easily left Hamblin there and continued the race. After all, this was the race she had prepared eight years to run.

Yet Abbey has a different view of competition. The kind of perspective that upholds the Olympic creed: "The most important thing in the Olympic Games is not to win but to take part, just as the most important thing in life is not the triumph but the struggle. The essential thing is not to have conquered but to have fought well."

When she saw Hamblin on the ground, Abbey told her, "Get up, get up. We have to finish this."

She then helped Hamblin to her feet, even though Abbey was injured herself. Though she didn't know it at the time, she had torn her anterior cruciate ligament and meniscus and strained the medial collateral ligament in her right knee.

After she had helped Hamblin up, Abbey started to run. Her injured knee buckled, and she collapsed to the ground. This time Hamblin helped her to get back on her feet. Then the two began to run again.

Abbey endured the pain and hobbled around the track. She *finished* the race 17 minutes and 10 seconds later—in last place. In doing so, she touched the hearts of people all over the world.

At the finish line, she was met with a wheelchair and an awestruck Hamblin.

"You suddenly get this sense that you are watching something incredible unfolding, and you wonder how to put it into words," said NBC commentator Tim Hutchings. "Her dream was crushed, but then magic happened. She will be a national hero now, an Olympic hero, and rightly so. She showed how a special act can reach people far more than all the medals in the world."[1]

"She did pretty much the opposite of what I told her," coach Mark Coogan told *USA Today*. "And I am so glad she did."[2]

Coogan was Abbey's cross-country coach at Dartmouth, where he had been impressed by her work ethic and her kindness. Under Coogan's coaching, Abbey became the most decorated athlete in Ivy League history. The two had often discussed what she should do if she fell during a race.

"I always told her, 'If you go down, here is what I want you to do,'"

Coogan told *USA Today*. "I told her to get up, dust herself off, have a quick look around, and then get right back to running. Obviously, she did pretty much the opposite of that, and the world got to see the kind of person she is. She did the right thing."[3]

Abbey is known by those close to her for always doing the right thing. At her training group with New Balance, the rest of the team, when facing challenges, often asks aloud, "What would Abbey do?"

They all hope that if presented with similar circumstances to that which Abbey faced on the Rio track that day, they would do what she did.

While most Olympic athletes spend a lifetime preparing for one brief moment to reach for the ultimate crown, it seems Abbey had prepared a lifetime for her one moment in just the way it unfolded.

"Although my actions were instinctual at that moment, the only way I have rationalized it is that God prepared my heart to respond that way," she said. "This whole time here He's made it clear to me that my experience in Rio was going to be about more than my race performance—and as soon as Nikki got up, I knew that was it."

Abbey's early years in running were different. She was focused solely on accomplishments and success. She was driven by a belief that she was lacking and had to earn acceptance. The result was burnout. She was beset by anxiety and panic attacks, and she was desperate for peace.

"I knew I had a natural love for running, but I felt a disconnect between my external and internal world," Abbey said. "I think that's what really led me to question, to seek God."

The peace she found has been noticeable to all. After winning a race, Abbey has been known to check on teammates who were still running or who had finished farther back and offer encouragement.

"God has taken me on an unparalleled journey," Abbey told Athletes in Action. "There have been a lot of ups and downs, but I would not have been able to learn any of the lessons, and I would never have reached such a familiarity and understanding of Christ without the way that it's happened."[4]

Going into the Rio race, Abbey believed that honoring God might not look the way she had expected. "[Honoring God] doesn't manifest in medals all the time," she said. "Sometimes it does, but it doesn't always. Sometimes it means coming in in last place."

After the Rio games, Abbey was in demand to tell her story. On *The Today Show* and numerous others she shared how she believes her athletic career unfolded in this way for a reason. Then she had surgery to repair her knee.

"It's useful to think about your purpose and become grounded in your identity beyond being a runner," she said. "My heart is so fickle, and the only times I've learned something in a transformative way are through these injuries. And when you think about them that way, it's like, 'Bring it on.'"

Abbey has her sights set on another goal: a PhD in psychology so she can help people (of course).

Just as she did that day in Rio for Hamblin, who said afterward, "I'm never going to forget that moment."

Neither will I. Nor will millions of others.

CLINT DEMPSEY

> » FACTOIDS

He played two matches in 2004 with a broken jaw.

He released a rap song titled "Don't Tread."

America's greatest soccer player was discovered by accident.

Born in Nacogdoches, Texas, Dempsey spent much of his childhood living in a trailer park. He and his siblings developed their soccer skills while playing with a large number of Hispanic immigrants who lived nearby.

"My parents had started me in the sport to help me learn good people skills," Dempsey said.

When his older brother, Ryan, was offered a tryout for an elite youth soccer club, the Dallas Texans, he brought Clint along. During Ryan's tryout, ten-year-old Clint passed the time by juggling a ball on the sideline. His skills were noticed by the club officials, who recruited Clint to play with them. The rest is history.

History as in the history Dempsey has made by becoming the leading international goal scorer in U.S. history, when he scored his fifty-seventh goal to tie former teammate Landon Donovan in 2017.

He has been a key member of the U.S. Men's National Team since 2004, playing on three World Cup teams. He is the only American ever to score a goal in three World Cups. In 2016 Fox Sports placed him at the top of the list of the greatest 50 players in USMNT history. In 2017 ESPN

FC named him the greatest soccer player in U.S. history. Major League Soccer also gave him that ranking the same year.

Dempsey's career would not have happened without his parents' willingness to drive.

Once the Texans recruited him to their youth club, it meant someone was going to have to get him to practice and games.

Dallas is a three-hour drive from Nacogdoches—one way. For more than a decade Dempsey's parents made the drive. They went through four cars and racked up more than 250,000 miles on those trips. They briefly tried a motor home to make it work.

Dempsey quickly became a standout for the Texans, but he had to quit due to his family's time and money constraints—and the fact that much of their time and money were going toward his older sister, Jennifer, who had become a highly ranked youth tennis player.

To help, several parents of Clint's teammates offered to assist the Dempseys with expenses and travel. This allowed him to rejoin the club.

Then tragedy struck the close Catholic family.

"When I was 12 years old, my life took a turn that would change me forever," Dempsey said. "My sister died [from a brain aneurysm] and I was faced with questions about why things happen and what role God played in it all. For a number of years, I struggled and put distance between God and me."

While Jennifer's death chilled his faith, it gave the devastated Dempsey a deeper motivation to pursue soccer in honor of his sister.

Dempsey went on to become the captain and highest scorer for the Texans, and he earned a scholarship to Furman University. His college experience also served to close the gap in his faith that had existed since his sister's death.

"In college, I joined a team Bible study. God's Word brought me peace and a desire for a relationship with Him," Dempsey told Athletes in Action. "I found that questioning Him and searching for answers through Scripture helped me grow and gave me direction. Now my faith in Christ is what gives me confidence for the future. I know that through both good times and bad, He is faithful and will watch over me…Little did I know that the sport I loved and the skills I learned would later play a role in my relationship with God."[1]

After Furman, Dempsey turned pro in 2004 at the age of 21 and played for the New England Revolution of Major League Soccer. He was selected as the MLS Rookie of the Year. That was the same year he made his first national team.

After scoring 25 goals in 71 games with New England, Dempsey joined Fulham in the English Premier League. From 2007 through 2012, Dempsey became the club's highest Premier League goal scorer of all time. He also became the first American player to score a hat trick in EPL play. He was twice voted Fulham's player of the season.

In 2012 Tottenham signed Dempsey for $9.6 million, a record contract for an American at the time. With Tottenham, Dempsey scored 12 goals, giving him a total of 72 goals scored across all competitions for Premier League clubs—the most ever by an American in the Premier League or any top league. He became the first American ever to play in a European final.

In 2013 Dempsey made the decision to return to the United States, signing a four-year contract with the Seattle Sounders for a transfer fee of $9 million, which made him the league's highest paid player.

He led Seattle to the MLS Cup final in 2014 and has been named the U.S. Soccer Male Athlete of the Year three times. Yet Dempsey's biggest moments have come with the U.S. national team in international competition.

In 2009 he scored against Egypt, Spain, and Brazil and led the United States into the FIFA Confederation Cup final. In 2010 he scored the tying goal against England in the World Cup opening game. In 2012 his goal gave the United States its first win in 78 years over Italy at an exhibition in Genoa. In 2015 he scored seven goals at the CONCACAF Gold Cup, helping the United States win the tournament.

Dempsey is one of the most dangerous attacking players the U.S. team has ever seen, and he's known for his dribbling tricks and movement on and off the ball, which have consistently created scoring opportunities for him and his teammates wherever he has played.

"Anytime you step on the field with him, you know he's going to be ready to give everything he has to the team to try and make a difference," U.S. team captain Michael Bradley told the *Dallas Morning News*.[2]

"You keep that same mentality and try to set the tone by your actions rather than by always speaking," Dempsey told the Dallas paper. "While you're playing, you try to enjoy it and have fun and make the most of it. I've enjoyed my career, and hopefully there's a little bit more time left."[3]

No one was quite sure how much time there might be for Dempsey when he was diagnosed in 2016 with an irregular heartbeat. His heart palpitations lasted for months. Yet months of testing did not find the cause. While Dempsey continued playing, doctors implanted a chip in his chest to collect data in an effort to figure out what was wrong.

"Then in one game," Dempsey said, "they saw something."

Months of signals from an irregular heartbeat finally showed up on the heart monitor.

"When they put the monitor in and were able to figure out what the problem was, that was kind of the most reassuring thing—that it's not going to affect your life," Dempsey said. "You know, I'm married with four kids, and the most important thing for me is family."

The health issue caused him to miss the 2016 Sounders season and the beginning of qualifying play for the 2018 World Cup. It also reminded him of a lesson he had learned when his sister died.

"Obviously things happen in your life along the way," he told the *New York Times*. "I remember growing up, losing a sister and—life is short. Make the most of your opportunities."[4]

Two medical procedures solved the irregular heartbeat, and Dempsey got back on the field in 2017, thankful the scare was not worse. Still, the experience with his own mortality has put things in perspective.

"I'm at peace with what I've been able to accomplish, not only domestically, but abroad, and what I was able to do on the international level," Dempsey said. "Being able to be a kid for that long period of time, being able to do something that you love…Those are things I'm going to think about.

"God provides strength even when circumstances seem impossible. Today, I pray for strength to walk the road before me. I play to the best of my abilities, and I am thankful for the many opportunities and amazing successes He has given me. Through it all, I want to do right, not make mistakes, and live a life that is pleasing to Him."

"A gem is not polished without friction."

CHINESE PROVERB

MONTY WILLIAMS

> **»FACTOIDS**

His roommate with the New York Knicks was Heisman Trophy winner Charlie Ward.

As an NBA player, he played for coaches Pat Riley and Greg Popovich.

Tragedy does not discriminate. Professional sports figures are not immune to its effect. Neither are good people. Trials visit everyone, and the response to them tells us so much about an individual.

Monty Williams had enjoyed a successful career as a player and coach in the NBA and a relatively normal family life when tragedy visited him in 2016, while he was a coach with the Oklahoma City Thunder.

On February 9, Williams's wife of 20 years, Ingrid, was driving on an Oklahoma City highway when an SUV crossed into her lane after the driver lost control and struck her car head-on. Ingrid died the next day from injuries suffered in the crash. In a moment, life was forever changed for the Williams family.

A week later Williams had the challenge of eulogizing his wife at a celebration of life service for Ingrid at Crossings Community Church in Oklahoma City. The event was attended by more than 900 people and broadcast worldwide by the NBA Network. Williams's response to the tragedy was remarkable.

"I'm thankful for all the people who showed up today," Williams told the audience. "It's a pretty tough time not just for me but for all of you as well. I'm mindful of that.

"This is hard for my family, but this will work out. And my wife would punch me if I were to sit up here and whine about what is going on. That doesn't take away the pain, but it will work out because God causes all things to work out. You just can't quit. You can't give in.

"God will work this out. My wife is in heaven. God loves us. God is love. And when we walk away from this place today, let's celebrate. Because my wife is where we all need to be. And I'm envious of that. But I got five crumb-snatchers I've got to deal with. I love you guys for taking time out of your day to celebrate my wife. We didn't lose her. When you lose something, you can't find it. I know exactly where my wife is. I'll miss holding her hand. I'll miss talking with my wife."

In the most moving part of his speech, Williams asked the audience to pray for the family of Susannah Donaldson, the driver of the other vehicle, who also died. Donaldson was traveling at 92 mph in a 45-mph zone when the accident occurred.

"Everybody is praying for me and my family, and that is right, but let us not forget that there were two people in this situation, and that family needs prayer as well," Williams stated. "And we have no ill will toward that family. In my house, we have a sign that says, 'As for me and my house, we will serve the Lord.' We cannot serve the Lord if we don't have a heart of forgiveness.

"That family didn't wake up wanting to hurt my wife. Life is hard. Life is very hard. And that was tough. But we hold no ill will towards the Donaldson family. And we, as a group, brothers united in unity, should be praying for that family because they grieve as well. So let's not lose sight of what is important."

Numerous NBA players, coaches, and executives attended the funeral to pay their respects and to support Williams, who played nine years in the league before coaching with San Antonio, New Orleans, Portland, and Oklahoma City. Among those present were Chris Paul, Tim Duncan, David West, Doc Rivers and his son Austin, and Anthony Davis. They were moved by Williams's display of forgiveness.

"If you know Monty, you're a better person for knowing him," West told ESPN after the funeral. "It's a really tough situation for his family. He's a courageous man. I envy his strength and his courage. That was probably one of the most powerful moments of my life, sitting there [and] listening to him have the strength to stand in front of his children and ask everybody to pray for the other lady that lost her life. It showed strength and courage I've never experienced in my life."[1]

"I told him he ain't always got to be the strong one," Paul said. "He's all about family, strong in his faith. You could see from the outpouring how strong he is and how much he's loved. We all could learn something from him."

"I just told him we all love him," Austin Rivers added.

The remarkable display of selflessness and forgiveness was not common, for sure. Nor was it a response that would have been expected from Williams when he was a budding All-American at Notre Dame 25 years earlier. In fact, it was another visit with trials back then that first changed his perspective.

Williams was planning on using college as a means to his future—either in the NBA or in the corporate world.

"Basketball—the status, notoriety, and desires that came with it—had become my god," he told *Sharing the Victory* magazine. "If anything fit my pursuit of being a great basketball player and making a bunch of money, then I'd do it.

"I had no idea that God had other plans in mind for me."[2]

Williams was planning on entering the NBA draft after his sophomore year at Notre Dame. Those plans were quickly dashed when a routine physical at the start of his sophomore year discovered that Williams had hypertrophic cardiomyopathy. The heart disease brought Williams's career to a sudden halt after just one season.

Williams turned to Ingrid, whom he had met during his first few weeks on campus. They had already developed a special relationship.

"The first thing out of her mouth was, 'Jesus can heal your heart,'" Williams said. "I'd read all the Bible stories in the past and had listened to a bunch of sermons in church about God, but they were just talks to me. I never really took them as truth.

"It was at that time that the Lord started to do some things in my heart that were really important," Williams continued. "As much as I needed my physical heart to be healed, my emotional heart needed it even more—and it all started with that one sentence Ingrid said to me when I told her about my heart condition."

Still, for two years Williams grew angrier and angrier about losing the opportunity to play the game he loved.

"It's a dangerous place to be," Williams said. "If you don't know that every gift comes from God, and you think that it comes from you—then you become your own god.

"I believed for two years that God would heal my heart," Williams said. "For two years nothing happened, so I just continued to go to class and continued to believe that, one day, God would heal my heart."

As his relationship with Ingrid deepened, Williams's perspective continued to change. He laid down the desire to play basketball and turned his focus on a future without the game.

Then, as he was preparing to graduate, Williams received a call from an athletic department staffer who suggested he undergo a series of tests at the National Institutes of Health. Williams agreed to do so.

After three days of scrutiny, doctors told Williams they couldn't find anything wrong with his heart.

"The power of prayer is amazing," he said. "I had so many people praying for me…When I got the good news, my mom was at the hospital, so we called Ingrid. All of us were crying together, so thankful that I'd get a chance to play again."

Williams played two more years at Notre Dame, earning honorable mention All-American honors in his final season after averaging 22.4 points and 8.4 rebounds per game. He was the New York Knicks first-round draft choice in the 1994 NBA draft. Just as Williams had planned, albeit later than expected.

Williams and Ingrid married after his rookie season. He was then traded to the San Antonio Spurs during his second season, getting him out of New York, which helped stabilize the young couple.

"That trade ended up being the best thing that happened to our marriage," Williams said. "At the time, I wasn't ready to be a mature husband. I still thought it was all about me, since I was the NBA athlete, and I was the one making the money."

The Williamses set down roots in a local church and surrounded themselves with mature people who could mentor them. Williams eventually realized basketball could never fill the God-sized void in his life.

"God showed me He had a purpose for my life that was far bigger than basketball, but that basketball could be a vehicle for me to share Him with others," Williams said. "After that, basketball wasn't who I was, but it was part of the total package I could become. It's just a testament to what God can do. I don't care what your situation is—God can change any heart. I'm 'Exhibit A' of that."

Over nine seasons Williams battled injuries while playing for Denver, Orlando, and Philadelphia after playing two key seasons in San Antonio and then retiring in 2003. He knew he wanted to stay in the game, so he joined the staff of the Spurs as a coaching intern. Then it was on to Portland as an assistant. In 2010 he was named the head coach of the New Orleans Hornets. While in OKC, he also served as an assistant coach for Team USA Basketball under Mike Krzyzewski, and that team ended up winning gold at the 2016 Rio Olympic Games. In 2016 he took on the role of vice president of basketball operations with the Spurs.

Through all his stops, Williams became a friend to many, which is the reason for the turnout at Ingrid's funeral and the reason Williams was honored with the inaugural Sager Strong Award for courage at the NBA Awards in June 2017. In receiving the award, and with his five children in attendance, Williams again demonstrated the perspective he has gained as he spoke of his wife's death.

"The good Lord in His sovereignty has trusted me and my family with our situation," Williams said. "I'm mindful of that. I'm mindful of all the blessings He's given me. For 20-plus years I've had the NBA family to support me, criticize me, and make me a better man."

He closed his speech by addressing his five children: Lael, Faith, Janna, Elijah, and Micah.

"I want you to know that you're not a job," Williams said. "I am honored to take care of you. The Bible says you are a blessing, and you have been. The reason I get up and do what I do is because of you all."

As Williams reflects back on the difficult journey, he remains thankful for what he has experienced and how the challenges have been used to have an impact on others.

"God has called me to serve right where I am," he said. "He's called me to be obedient, show up on time, and do my job to the absolute best of my abilities. In the midst of that, He has used me to do some things I know I couldn't do on my own."

"Teamwork is the ability to work together toward a common vision; the ability to direct individual accomplishments toward organizational objectives. It is the fuel that allows common people to attain uncommon results."

—ANDREW CARNEGIE

company service
alliance working together

TEAMWORK

combination
collaboration teaming
society unity synergy
combination
partnership

"As the challenge escalates, the need for teamwork elevates."

JOHN MAXWELL

ALLYSON FELIX

She is a young woman going somewhere fast—always.

Allyson Felix is one of the greatest female sprinters in history. For more than a decade she has lived with constant comparisons to the greats of eras past while running past every opponent in the world on her way to virtual dominance of her generation.

She is a nine-time Olympic medalist, making her the most decorated female track-and-field athlete in Olympic history. Six of her Olympic medals are gold. She's the first female track and field athlete ever to achieve that. She has won 17 medals at the World Championships, 12 of them gold. Yet she is perhaps the most humble and unassuming star the sport has ever seen.

"Allyson didn't run track until basically ninth grade," said her father, Paul Felix. "That was the first time she put on track shoes."

"She tried out for the track team, and the coach thought his stopwatch was broken, so he had her go back and try again," recalls Allyson's mother, Marlean. "I think she was running in these big basketball shoes, but he pointed out she was just so quick."

Allyson went from those basketball shoes at L.A. Baptist High School to the Olympic Games in Athens, Greece, in a three-year period. Talk about quick. The road to the big stage was filled with the diminutive Felix's startling rise to elite status.

When she was a ninth grader, Allyson made it to the California high school state finals. In the tenth grade, she won the state title in the 100 meters. And by the twelfth grade she started competing with some of the world's finest athletes.

"She was 17 and she's running against some 25-year-olds," said Marlean. "For track and field, 24 and 25 seems to be the prime for women, and here she was beating them."

Allyson stunned the track-and-field world by running to a silver medal in the 200 meters at the 2004 Olympics in Athens when she was 18 years old. She also broke the world junior record in the event. A year later, at age 19, she won the world championship. It was clear that the teen from California had arrived—fast.

"When they put that wreath on her head and when they hung that medal around her neck, it all came together," said her mother. "And I have flashes of her on the track—all that she had gone through to reach this point at such a tender age—and the emotions just overtook me."

"I think just receiving my medal, I just felt really proud," said Allyson. "I think when I initially had finished the race I was disappointed [in finishing second], but through my family's help they helped me put everything into perspective, and I think at that time I was able to see what I had accomplished and see the [short] amount of time it took me.

"I definitely feel like I've been blessed with this gift, and so that's something that helps me to see the bigger picture," she told the *Los Angeles Times*. "It's so easy to get caught up in winning everything and just the kind of the grind of what professional sports is, but faith leads my life, and it definitely helps me to kind of pull back and see that there's a greater purpose."[1]

Later Allyson again experienced a sense of momentary disappointment. At the 2008 Olympics in Beijing she won gold in the 4x400 relay but was unable to take home an individual gold, again winning silver in the 200, leaving her frustrated that her golden moment had not yet come. After coming in second in 2004 and 2008, she wept. The weight of unfulfilled expectations had become burdensome.

"I think a lot of times you want faith to kind of be the answer to everything, and it's still a struggle to get there, you know? There are very real moments that are hard, but I think it helps me to be able to learn the lesson that there is a purpose, a reason why maybe that happened, and it can create something in you, and it might be preparing you for something better in the future," Allyson said.

"I try not to focus on the pressure…I love [the Bible verse] Philippians 4:6-7 that says, 'Do not be anxious about anything, but in everything, by prayer and petition, with thanksgiving, present your requests to God. And the peace of God, which transcends all understanding, will guard your hearts and your minds in Christ Jesus.' That verse always calms my heart."

It's not as though Allyson had not experienced success. She won gold in the 200 at the world championships in 2005, 2007, and 2009, identifying her as the best in the world. Still, she maintained she would trade all three of those medals for one Olympic gold. She was determined that the 2012 Olympics would be her time. And it was.

She won gold in the 200 at the 2012 London games with a time of 21.88. After a decade of chasing the perfect 22 seconds, she found it.

"The moments that motivated me the most were losing on the biggest stage and never forgetting that feeling," she told the press after her victory. "Now I'm able to say that I embrace that journey because that is what has pushed me all these years."

After finally chasing down her goal, Allyson remained gracious and humble. She strolled deliberately around the track, stopping along the way to hold up a U.S. flag. When she spotted her family in the stands, she made her way to them to share a moment that was not about her but about her family. "It was just complete happiness," she told the press.

"We've tried to train her not to bring the attention to herself," said her father. "So very rarely would she show emotions when she wins a race. She'll never be the kind of individual who pumps up her hand with number one or anything like that."

"Everyone is always watching you and everything that you do," Allyson agreed. "So I feel like that's your best opportunity to really show what you're about."

A support system is critical for most athletes. Much of Allyson's grounding comes through the closeness of her family. Her father has been a mentor and has helped Allyson set her life on a solid foundation. Her brother Wes has been part training partner and part cheerleader. He also became her agent in 2012.

"They really have a special relationship," Paul said of Allyson's close bond with her brother. "He's a big brother. He spoils her and watches over her and takes care of her."

Once a promising runner himself, Wes has served as a voice of wisdom for Allyson. His role has been to protect her from outside forces, steer her in the right direction, and handle the distractions so she can focus on what happens on the track.

"I always want to be there for her, and I think that's the best way I can be an older brother," said Wes.

Her family was one of the main reasons the disappointments of 2004 and 2008 did not crush Allyson. The support system was there to encourage her and help her set her sights on the next opportunity.

"I am so blessed to have my family and the upbringing that I did," she said. "It means so much to me to have two very godly parents who both have so much wisdom. They are amazing role models that I have had the privilege to watch as I grew up."

Her support system pushed Allyson beyond her 2012 gold. At the 2016 games in Rio, she once again was faced with trial and triumph.

A hamstring injury left her unable to compete for a spot in the 200, meaning she had to give up the opportunity to defend her Olympic title as well as the dream of running for the gold in both the 200 and 400 meters. She turned her attention to the 400 and the relays.

In a crowning moment to her illustrious career, Allyson won silver in the 400 and gold in both the 4x100 and 4x400 relays, giving her 36 medals in international competition and making her the most dominant female track star of her era. And in an age where doping has almost become a foregone conclusion, Allyson has achieved it all by competing clean.

Somewhat diminutive by sprinter standards, Allyson is five feet six. Yet her lithe stature belies her strength. In high school, she deadlifted more than 270 pounds.

Knowing the scrutiny that successful sprinters face, in 2008 Allyson decided to take part in a new drug-testing program. She volunteered to submit to a significant number of random tests, which were both uncomfortable and inconvenient. Yet Allyson knew that her actions could help bring credibility back to the sport and allow her to demonstrate the values she has based her life on.

"I just felt like whatever I can do to prove I'm clean, no matter what time I have to wake up or where I have to drive, I'm willing," she told the *Los Angeles Times*. "I feel more responsible myself to be a role model for younger kids…that's important to me.

"I'm trying to make a name for myself, and I hope that people can distinguish the character and the way I present myself."[2]

Her parents are understandably proud of their daughter's approach.

"She's just trying to be the best that God would want her to be," said Marlean.

"I'm currently a work in progress, and like anyone else I face struggles every day," Allyson said. "You have to have a passion, and you have to have a reason for doing what you're doing, and there really has to be a purpose there. I think that's what drives success. I know my talent is from God. And that's my purpose: to run to glorify Him."

> *"Talent wins games, but teamwork and intelligence wins championships."*
>
> **MICHAEL JORDAN**

LAURIE HERNANDEZ

»FACTOIDS

She collects keychains from all of her travels for competition.

During training, she eats oatmeal and fruit for breakfast every day.

As a 16-year-old, Laurie Hernandez participated in the biggest competition of her life. She stared down the world's biggest platform and performed like a veteran.

As a member of the U.S. women's gymnastics team at the 2016 Rio Olympics, Hernandez looked the part of an ice-in-the-veins veteran, nailing her routines and tumbling her way into history.

She was the youngest member of Team USA that won the Women's Gymnastics Team All-Around gold medal by more than eight points—the largest margin of victory in Olympic gymnastics history.

The women of this team were called the "Final Five" because they were the last group under the tutelage of legendary coach Márta Károlyi: Aly Raisman, Gabby Douglas, Madison Kocian, Simone Biles, and Hernandez. Their win was startling, not in that they accomplished it, but rather by the score in a sport normally determined by tenths of a point. The performance will make this group long remembered as one of the greatest collections of gymnasts in history.

If Biles was the standout, Raisman the steady one, and Douglas the veteran influence, it was Hernandez who was the spark. She exuded joy throughout the night. Her constant smile seemed to bring a relief to her teammates from the weight of expectations. Yet it was her performance as much as her easy nature that boosted the team.

Hernandez led off the competition with a strong vault, went on to perform a nearly flawless beam routine, and then brought the crowd to their feet with her floor routine.

Before the night was over, Hernandez went on to win a silver medal in the individual balance beam event, showing the courage that helped her win a spot on the team. A fall from the beam in 2014 produced Hernandez's first serious injuries, a fractured wrist and a dislocated kneecap. The medal in Rio was a testament to her willingness to face fear and overcome it.

"I've been training so hard, so I'm glad I just did the routine I've been doing in practice, and I have no regrets," Hernandez said in an interview on *The Today Show*. "I kind of thought I was going to throw up before I went. My coach said, 'That was the most nervous I've ever seen you before a meet,' but then once I got on the beam I was actually calmer than I usually am."[1]

After leaving the team medal stand, adorned with gold around her neck at the end of the night, she made eye contact with her parents, who were cheering from the crowd. She held up her medal to them and flashed her famous smile, sharing the moment with the ones who were most responsible for her being there.

The smile, the personality, and the performance made Hernandez a national hit. In the aftermath, she did the talk show circuit; appeared on *Sesame Street*, *Stuck in the Middle*, and at the Macy's Thanksgiving Day Parade; and wrote an autobiography, *I Got This: To Gold and Beyond*.

For good measure, she was selected to participate in *Dancing with the Stars* in 2016, partnering with Val Chmerkovskiy to win the competition and becoming the youngest celebrity to do so.

None of this is a surprise to those who know Hernandez well. Her personality mixed with a calm tenaciousness makes Hernandez so appealing both on and off the gymnastics mat. Her expressive face and exuberance have earned her the nickname "the Human Emoji."

"I'm still a goof. I'm really silly," said Hernandez. "Even though I'm goofy, I'm still very spiritual and one with God."

It's this ability to be both light and serious that makes her so unique.

Quick to laugh and often entertaining, Hernandez is an uncommon mix of charisma and grit. She is a blue-collar kid in a ribbons-and-bows world. It's part of her New Jersey upbringing with traditional values instilled by her parents. Her mother, Wanda, is a social worker who has also served in the army reserves. Her father, Anthony, is a court officer in New Jersey.

Hernandez is also buoyed by her family's heritage. Of Puerto Rican descent, Hernandez became just the fourth Latina to represent the U.S. in gymnastics in the last 80 years.

"I'm just proud of my heritage," Hernandez said in an interview with NBC. "I think it's amazing that I can just go out there and be myself, and the fact that I'm carrying Puerto Rico on my back a little bit, I think that's an honor."[2]

Hernandez first caught the attention of the national women's gymnastics elite as an 11-year-old. She became the junior national all-around silver medalist in 2013 in only her second year in that echelon of competition. By 2016 she was hailed as a breakout star in her first year at the senior level.

"We go into 2016, and obviously I've realized that this is an Olympic year…I have been training my whole life for this," she recalled. "So I noticed I was definitely stressed as soon as the year hit.

"My mom could tell. She was like, 'What's on your mind? Why are you so tense? You've seemed really built up lately?' I was like, 'Well, I'm scared.' I'm like 'Come on, Mom, it's an Olympic year. Don't you get it? Like, this is a big deal?…I want to make the team. As a little kid this is all I ever wanted.' She was like, 'You still don't control the future.' And then I thought, *Yeah, you're right. I don't.*"[3]

The realization changed Laurie's mental approach, which released the fear.

"I'm coming in, training as hard as I can," she recalled. "If I make it, that would be amazing, but if I don't, then that's a different path God wants me to take, and I know that there are better and greater things God wants me to do."[4]

Hernandez was no stranger to nerves, which plagued her as a child. Through her faith, she learned how to deal with the anxiety.

"I just wake up thanking God for another day and go to sleep thanking God for another day," she said. "Sometimes things just don't work out, and so you just gotta let God push you through those rough times.

"Usually, before I salute the judge, I'm able to just grab the event and I pray on it, and that really grounds me," she continued. "And for some reason, once I do that, I am able to think clearly and calm down right before I compete."[5]

She says that accomplishing that which is beyond her comfort level is what makes all the sacrifices and long hours of practice worth it.

"I think it's just a mini-battle with myself," she said. "I think I want to prove to myself that even on the rough days when I thought I couldn't do it, I did it anyway."[6]

The teen who not only likes to conquer the biggest mountains but also likes to draw and write poetry is anchored in it all by her faith.

"I feel that, every day, God molds me into someone that He wants me to be," she said. "So if that means just, like, talking to teammates and helping them out, or, like, every so often I'll post a Bible verse on Twitter or Instagram."[7]

A post she made on Twitter in the aftermath of the Olympics seems to speak volumes about this five-foot gymnast with the giant-sized character: "In the happy moments, praise God. In the hard times, seek God. In the quiet moments, trust God. In every moment, thank God."[8]

"Sticks in a bundle are unbreakable."

KENYAN PROVERB

DICK AND RICK HOYT

»FACTOIDS

Rick is a huge Boston Bruins fan.

Rick's first "spoken" words by computer were "Go Bruins!"

They are *the* endurance sport family, and they are truly amazing.

Dick and Rick Hoyt are a father-and-son team who together have competed in just about every endurance race they have been able to find over the past 40 years. If they have not been competing in a marathon on any given weekend, it means they have been entered in a triathlon instead. Whether 26.2 miles of running in the former or 26.2 miles of running, 112 miles of bicycling, and 2.4 miles of swimming in the latter, the Hoyts have done it together.

Together. It is the word that most easily identifies this father-son team. They have become a model of endurance and a symbol of love. Together.

You see, Rick can't run. Or bike. Or swim. In fact, he can't walk or talk. He is confined to a wheelchair. For the past 40 years, Rick's father, Dick, has pushed and pulled his son across the country and over thousands of finish lines. They are a father and son bonded by challenge and sport, supporting each other through tests of human endurance. It is an uncommon blend of a son's joy and a father's love, and it is quite a sight to see.

When Dick runs, he pushes Rick in a wheelchair. When Dick cycles, Rick sits in a wheelchair attached to the front of the bike. When Dick swims, he pulls Rick in a small stabilized boat. On land and water, they carry on.

Rick was born in 1962 with the umbilical cord coiled around his neck, which cut off the oxygen flow to his brain. Doctors told Dick and his wife, Judy, there was no hope for Rick's development.

"It's been a story of exclusion ever since he was born," Dick said. "When he was eight months old, the doctors told us we should just put him away, that he'd be a vegetable all his life. Well, those doctors are not alive any more, but I would like them to be able to see Rick now."

The Hoyts held on to the fact that Rick's eyes followed them around the room, which gave them hope that he would somehow be able to communicate someday. Every week the Hoyts took Rick to Children's Hospital in Boston, where they met a doctor who encouraged them to treat Rick like any other child.

Convinced Rick was every bit as intelligent as his two younger brothers, the Hoyts determined to raise him as normally as possible. Local school authorities, however, didn't agree with the parents' assessment.

"Because he couldn't talk, they thought he wouldn't be able to understand, but that wasn't true," said Dick, a retired lieutenant colonel in the Air National Guard.

So the Hoyts taught Rick the alphabet themselves. Judy spent hours each day teaching him with sandpaper letters and by posting signs on everything in the house. In a short amount of time, Rick learned the alphabet.

Through the efforts of some Tufts University engineers, Rick was equipped at age 11 with an interactive computer that enabled him to communicate by using slight head movements to highlight letters and spell out words. Within a brief time, Rick was "writing" out his thoughts and communicating clearly. When he was 13 years old and with the aid of this device, he was able to attend a public school for the first time.

Two years later Rick heard about a five-mile road race to benefit a lacrosse player from his school who had become paralyzed. Driven by his deep sense of compassion, Rick told his dad he wanted them to participate—together. There was one problem with the plan: Dick was not a runner.

Great love requires great sacrifice. Dick, then 36 years old, determined this sacrifice was worth it. He agreed to participate and to push Rick in his wheelchair the entire five miles. The pair finished next to last, but after returning home from the race, Rick typed on his computer the words that changed both of their lives: "Dad, when I'm running, it feels like my disability disappears."

At that moment Team Hoyt was born.

Dick began running every day with a bag of cement in the wheelchair while Rick was at school and studying. He got into such good shape that, even while pushing his son, he achieved a personal record of a 5K run in 17 minutes.

Dick and Rick began to compete in more events. These competitions became the most meaningful experiences of Rick's life.

"What I mean when I say I feel like I am not handicapped when competing is that I am just like the other athletes," Rick said through his technology tools. "Now many athletes will come up to me before the race or triathlon to wish me luck."

Early on, that wasn't the case.

"Nobody wanted Rick in a road race," recalled Dick. "Everybody looked at us, but nobody talked to us. Nobody wanted to have anything to do with us. As time went on, though, they could see he was a person—he has a great sense of humor, for instance. That made a big difference."

After four years of marathons, Team Hoyt tackled triathlons. For this, Dick had to learn to swim.

"I sank like a stone at first," he said.

With a specially designed tandem bike adapted to carry Rick in front and with a small boat tied around Dick's waist by a rope as he swam, the Hoyts came in second to last in a competition held on Father's Day 1985. They have been competing ever since and inspiring those around them.

Since 1977 the Hoyts have competed in more than 1,100 endurance events, including more than 75 marathons and 7 Ironman triathlons. They have run the Boston Marathon more than 30 times. In 1992 they biked and ran across the United States, completing a full 3,735 miles in 45 days. Between 2004 and 2012 the father-son team was featured on inspirational billboards across the country.

For four decades Dick Hoyt has pushed his body to the limit of human capability, not for fame or riches, but simply for the joy of his son feeling free from his disability for a few hours.

"Dad is one of my role models," Rick said. "Once he sets out to do something, Dad sticks to it, whatever it is until it is done. For example, once we decided to really get into triathlons, Dad worked out, up to five hours a day, five times a week, even when he was working."

"Rick is the one who inspires and motivates me," Dick said. "People just need to be educated. Rick is helping many other families who are coping with disabilities in their struggle to be included."

Rick continually inspires. He graduated from high school and moved on to Boston University, where he earned a degree in special education. He also secured a job at the Boston College computer laboratory. There, Rick helped develop systems through which mechanical aids, such as a motorized wheelchair, can be controlled by eye movements when linked to a computer to better aid persons with disabilities with communication and independence.

In 2013 ESPN honored Team Hoyt with the Jimmy V Perseverance Award. Earlier that year a bronze statue in honor of the Hoyts was dedicated on April 8, 2013, near the start of the Boston Marathon in Hopkinton, Massachusetts.

That same year, after more than three decades of competition, Team Hoyt had to acknowledge that all these races had taken a physical toll on them. Dick, then 73, and Rick, then 52, decided to make the 2013 Boston Marathon—their favorite race—their last marathon competition. A terrorist bombing near the finish line, however, stopped the duo at the 23-mile mark, meaning they could not finish. So Dick and Rick decided to make the 2014 Boston Marathon their final race.

Since then Team Hoyt has competed in shorter races and triathlons. They are not close to finishing, because they are committed to inspiring people across America to know that nothing is impossible when people work together.

When asked if he could give his father one thing, Rick responded, "The thing I'd most like is for my dad to sit in the chair and I would push him for once."

JORDY NELSON

»FACTOIDS

Nelson's wife, Emily, played basketball at Bethel College.

He set his high school's records for steals, blocked shots, and assists in basketball.

Most professional athletes look forward to the day when their career is over and they can retire to a relaxed lifestyle, perhaps on a beach or on a boat, and live off their earnings.

Not Jordy Nelson.

The Green Bay Packers Pro Bowl receiver is looking forward to post-NFL career days when he and his family will embark on a different kind of work.

"I plan on taking my two boys and little girl back to Kansas and living on a farm when I'm done playing," Nelson said. "I envision our kids doing what I did when I was growing up—helping me on the farm and helping my brother, who does it now for a living with his family. I envision both of our families out there working together."

Nelson was raised in Riley, Kansas, population 992, tucked in the northeast part of Kansas. His family has been farming the land there and raising livestock for four generations, going back to his great-great-grandfather, who immigrated from Sweden. Nelson and his brother worked the farm when they were kids—two hours a day, driving a combine to cut wheat or rounding up the 1,000-cow herd—and they loved it.

"Growing up on a farm is all I knew," Nelson said. "It was a lot of work, but at the same time we had a lot of fun farming with my dad and grandpa and my older brother. It instilled a lot of things in me and shaped me into who I am today…the hard work, loyalty, just endless things."

Tending 200 head of Black Angus cattle and farming more than 1,000 acres was tiring work, especially during the summer when the sun was blistering and their workday started early and finished late.

"Come summertime, we were up by seven, eight o'clock, doing chores, harvesting wheat, working cattle, building fences, anything. It's an endless list."

It was on the farm that Nelson learned the valuable lessons that would prepare him for what was ahead in his athletic career.

"It's legitimately you reap what you sow," he said. "It was a lot of hard work, but once it came harvesttime, and once you were able to sell those crops or sell those cattle, you reaped the rewards of what you put in. It taught you patience because there could be some long days. You learned to appreciate what you put into it, that your quality of work mattered. If it wasn't right, you had to redo it. Go do it and do it right because it mattered. Every day was different, which was what I truly enjoyed about farming."

The experience also developed a unique sense of teamwork in the Nelson family, where the consequences were crucial to the family's future.

"The rest of my family was depending on each other," Nelson recalled. "I depended on my dad to make money to feed us. He depended on us to go out and get the work done so he could do the other things that were necessary to make a living. You had to pull your own weight."

The lessons learned and the character instilled helped turn Nelson from a walk-on safety at Kansas State to an All-American receiver and eventually to a second-round draft choice and an All-Pro.

"You're not going to reap the rewards from one day of working. You get better. With experience, you learn to do it the right way," Nelson said of the application of farming to football. "It's an everyday thing. It's the foundation of who I am. You learn to work, put the effort in, do it the right way, do it to the best of your ability."

That perspective, along with his six-foot-three, 217-pound frame, sprinter's speed, and glue-like hands, continues to keep Nelson among the elite receivers in the game. Opponents know that combination, along with the farmer's work ethic, make him a difficult matchup on the field.

"Jordy is a hardworking farm boy," former teammate Greg Jennings told *Sports Illustrated*. "His physical skill set is second to none, but he's smart, he works at his craft, he studies the game. He's a hardworking farm boy in his life, and he's a hardworking farm boy on the field."[1]

Over his first nine seasons with the Packers, Nelson has caught 550 passes for 69 touchdowns. He has seasons of catching 13, 14, and 15 touchdown passes, and seasons with 98, 97, and 85 receptions. When healthy, he is one of the most dangerous receivers in the game.

Nelson and quarterback Aaron Rodgers have a special connection. After countless hours of practice together, they are often able to read each other during a play and improvise on the field.

"It means we've been successful, and we've put in a lot of time," Nelson said. "It's a reminder to me of the time and work we've both put in individually and together on the practice field, in the meeting rooms, on the sideline, and just reaping the benefits for it."

"Body language, unspoken adjustments, eye contact—we've made a lot of hay on those things," Rodgers said. "We have really good chemistry on and off the field."[2]

Nelson enjoys similar chemistry with the fans in Green Bay. For this farm kid, life in the rural Green Bay area is comforting. There is even a pasture backing up to his home. Because of his success on the field and because he also holds their Midwest values, Packers fans love Nelson. The feeling is mutual.

"It's been a perfect fit for my family and me," he said. "The fan support—from the chaos at training camp with all the fans who come out, to when we go on the road and all the fans who travel to support us and you hear the 'Go Pack Go' chant—is amazing."

His success in Green Bay is a long way from Nelson's beginnings in Riley, Kansas. When Nelson and his brother weren't working on the farm, they were playing sports. Jordy's raw athleticism was fueled by his work ethic and produced a unique talent mix.

As a high school senior Nelson won the state championship in the 100 meters with a time only 15 other high school runners in America beat that year. He was also first-team All-State in basketball and second-team

All-State in football. Yet his performances for Riley County High, which had just 250 students in grades 9 through 12, made it hard for Nelson to get noticed by colleges.

Only Division-II schools Emporia State and Washburn showed any interest. So Nelson chose to be a walk-on at Kansas State.

While he had been a quarterback in high school, Nelson was converted to safety by coach Bill Snyder. Out of position, Nelson was eventually shifted to receiver. In his first season at the new position, he led the team with 45 catches, and as a senior, he caught 122 passes for 11 touchdowns and was named a consensus All-American. He left Kansas State holding 11 different receiving records.

The Packers saw a receiver who had great speed, was strong enough to fight off coverage at the line of scrimmage, had great hands, and would not be outworked. They made him the thirty-sixth overall selection in the 2008 draft.

Nelson's most memorable game in a Packers uniform may have been Super Bowl XLV, when he caught 9 passes for 140 yards and touchdown in Green Bay's 31–25 win over the Pittsburgh Steelers to cap the 2010 season. He scored the game's first touchdown, a 29-yard reception in the first quarter. It was the night the nation realized just how good Nelson is.

"Since that game, he's been our best receiver," said Rodgers. "He took a big confidence jump after that game."

Yet for all the rewards that performance and a Super Bowl championship brought him, Nelson has a perspective on that game that goes against the general perception.

"The Super Bowl gets built up so much. Don't get me wrong. It is the pinnacle of our career, but I definitely would not say it's the pinnacle of my life," Nelson said. "You can get caught up in it. You know, if you win the Super Bowl, it will change your life forever. If that's all you live for, if you're looking for that to change your life, you're going to fall short. You realize how quickly it moves on. You move on. Fans move on. The NFL moves on. Next year there's another Super Bowl winner, and it just continues.

"Obviously, it's nothing someone can take away from me in my career, but as a person it's a very small part of what I've accomplished."

Following the 2017 season, Nelson moved on too. The Packers, in an effort to cut costs, cut Nelson. After nine seasons in Green Bay, where he totaled 550 catches for nearly 8,000 yards and 69 touchdowns, Nelson was moving on. He was quickly signed by the Oakland Raiders. In exiting, Nelson shared a message with the Packers faithful via Twitter:

> Packers Fans, my family and I would like to say THANK YOU for your support over the last 10 yrs. We have been blessed to call Green Bay our home and WI will always be a part of our lives. We have many great memories and it's the people we will miss the most. Until next time.

Nelson says the money, the statistics, even the Super Bowl title can't compare to being a husband and father. His wife, Emily, also grew up on a farm, and the two first met in kindergarten.

"I've known my wife my whole life," Nelson said on Dan Le Batard's radio show. We grew up together—went to kindergarten together all the way through. We grew up three miles apart, which is not very far when you grew up out in the country in Kansas…We dated and then she dumped me…It was seventh grade. She had an incredible reason why— it was the end of the school year and it was summertime, and she didn't want to be tied down to one guy in seventh grade during the summer."

The two resumed their relationship during their freshman year in high school and were married in 2007. Like her husband, Emily enjoys the simple life and looks forward to moving back to a farm.

"My wife and I are both homebodies, so we'd rather be at home and hanging out with friends than going out on the town," Jordy said.

Home is where they raise their three kids, instilling the same values that were instilled in them.

"The biggest part is trying to keep my kids understanding the financial aspect we'll be in…that the money didn't just appear, and the fact that we are very blessed financially doesn't change anything—how you should work, what you need to do, how you should treat people…and it's not yours. It's Mom and Dad's," he said with a chuckle.

"I think that will be the biggest challenge, and that's another reason I want to move back. Going back home and making them work will build the kind of foundation I had."

As part of modeling that character, Jordy and Emily launched the

Nelson Family Community Foundation, which benefits families in need in his farming community in Kansas and supported Young Life, a Christian youth organization connecting area youth with Christ.

"Sometimes I wonder why God gave me the talent to play football and blessed me with this," Nelson said. "He keeps you humble and realistic in understanding what truly is important, what matters and how quickly it can be taken away.

"There is a bigger picture. Football is a very small part of our life. We're trying to understand why we've been given this platform and how we can make the most of it. Whether it's mentoring kids, being a role model, doing the right thing—how can we make the most of the opportunity we've been given? We've been put on this platform, and now what are we going to do with it?"

His faith and his Midwestern values keep Nelson grounded. It is so much of why he longs to return to farming. It is also why he is authentic. When he goes home to the Nelson farm in the summer, he still drives the same 2003 Chevy Silverado he bought while he was a student-athlete at Kansas State. He still helps to harvest the winter wheat crop before training camp begins.

"I probably identify more as a farmer than as a football player," he said. "[In Riley], I'm just the farm kid they have always known."

> *"Ask not what your teammates can do for you.*
> *Ask what you can do for your teammates."*

MAGIC JOHNSON

CHRIS PAUL

»FACTOIDS

As a youth, he worked at his grandfather's service station, rotating tires and changing air filters.

He owns a franchise in the Professional Bowlers Association.

Chris Paul has been one of the NBA's most exciting players over his 13-year career. Yet for all his greatness, the one thing that drives him—a championship—has eluded his grasp.

After six years in New Orleans, where Chris became an elite player, he moved to the Los Angeles Clippers in search of a title. Following six years in L.A. without a ring, Chris was on the move again, uniting with James Harden in Houston in 2017 to form the NBA's most lethal backcourt combo. In a career that has seen him put up nearly 19 points and 10 assists and more than 2 steals per game, Paul is on his way to the Hall of Fame.

A combination of offensive skills makes this point guard so difficult to defend. With his ability to create shots and penetrate, he is nearly unstoppable. He is fearless in taking the ball inside against the big men, can hit a jumper from almost anywhere on the court, and is consistently in double figures in assists. Opposing defenses know that, when he is on, they are in for a long night. Yet his defensive prowess is equally as impressive.

His all-around greatness is demonstrated in his numbers. He has led the league in both assists and steals. He has been named to the all-BBA team, the All-Star team, and the All-Defensive team multiple times. In a 2016 game against New Orleans, Chris registered 20 points, 20 assists, and no turnovers—the first player ever to do so in league history.

"I truly love my job," he said. "I get to wake up every morning and say, 'I play basketball for my living.'"

"He's a buzz saw on the court, and whenever he steps on the court it's business," said Charles Paul, Chris's father. "He wants to win."

"When I'm playing, I'm in a totally different world," said Chris. "On the court, nothing else in the world matters except for beating the other team and beating the other guy in front of me…When I'm on the court, it's all about the task at hand, and this is my battleground."

"He always had big dreams," said Chris's brother, C.J. "He'd never let anybody tell him he couldn't do something. Just like when he came in NBA. Some people said he was too small. I mean, he's proved so many people wrong, so many people wrong."

"I've just always been extremely, extremely competitive," said Chris. "When I walk onto the court, it could be the tallest man in the world, could be the shortest, and I'm gonna play the same way. That's just the way I've always been."

While he has become one of the elite players in the game—a star who single-handedly changes the game and forces opposing teams to game plan to stop him, Chris Paul is at heart a team player.

"Teamwork is everything, especially in basketball," he said. "Everything starts and ends with the point guard, offensively and defensively."

His commitment to team is why Chris has been searching to find the right chemistry for a championship. He is more interested in making those around him successful than in his own personal numbers.

"I start off the game the same way just about every time, and I get my teammates involved," Chris said. "I just score when I have to."

When he "has to" is more often than opponents would like, and often it comes in a circus variety. An array of highlight-reel shots has made him a fan favorite all over the world. Yet Chris continues to believe it is better to give than to receive.

"My favorite moment in a game is when I make a nice move and give it to one of my teammates and they score," said Chris. "When I see the excitement on their face, it makes me feel good to know that they're happy…and that makes me happy."

That spirit of teamwork began in Chris's childhood. His family developed a support network and protective system that continues today.

"I'm lucky in that I have a family that's always been there for me," Chris said. "Everyone who knows me may know my parents before they know me. My parents love basketball and they love sports, and I think that's where we bond even more.

"I know when my parents are at my games, they're not just there because I'm playing. They're there because they're basketball junkies. They want to see the game. They want to know what's happening. And they're there to support me."

"I thank God every day where He has all of us—my whole family—at this time in our life," said Charles. "Just watching Chris on the basketball court is an extension of God's love."

Through his family, Chris learned to succeed on and off the court and developed a foundation of faith—a faith that today is his source, keeps him grounded, and drives him.

"It's truly a privilege to be in the NBA, and I understand that it's nothing I've done," said Chris. "It's all by God's grace and Him giving me this opportunity to use basketball as a platform.

"I think, when you have God in your life, you feel like there's nobody who can touch you. To have that rock, that constant, there's no one—when you have that rock as Jesus Christ—who can take that away from you. When you know God as that rock and that foundation, then you always have somebody to call on...always."

"Every human being, of whatever origin,
of whatever station, deserves respect.
We must each respect others
even as we respect ourselves."

—U THANT

honor courtesy
gentleness
friendliness
RESPECT
appreciation
thoughtfulness adoration
regard esteem
graciousness dignity
consideration

> *"They cannot take away our self-respect*
> *if we do not give it to them."*
>
> **MAHATMA GANDHI**

KEVIN DURANT

» FACTOIDS

He grew five inches between his junior and senior years in high school.

Crab legs are his favorite food.

In sports, like life, decisions determine the outcomes that affect destiny. The decision Kevin Durant made in 2016, which was widely criticized, resulted in the outcome he had long desired: an NBA championship.

Durant has been one of the game's dominant scorers since he entered the league in 2007 as a 19-year-old fresh out of the University of Texas. At six-feet-nine, with a long wingspan and point guard–like ball skills, he is a nightmare matchup for defenders. Which is a big reason why he has averaged more than 27 points per game.

He became a star for the Oklahoma City Thunder. Seven times he was named an All-Star, and in 2014 he was voted the NBA's Most Valuable Player.

But for all the individual successes he realized, between the 2015–16 season and the 2016–17 season, Durant felt an emptiness. He wanted to win a championship. Durant's contract with the Thunder was up, and he started to consider his options. He loved OKC and had long imagined he'd spend his career there. Yet when the Thunder made decisions that seemed to move them further away from competing for a title, Durant began exploring opportunities that might give him a better chance of playing for a championship.

The Golden State Warriors were coming off a 2015–16 season in which they had won the most games in the history of the NBA yet blew the biggest lead in NBA Finals history and lost to the Cleveland Cavaliers. With a bitter taste in their mouths, the Warriors were looking for a key piece that would get them back to a championship.

A natural sports marriage was in order.

Durant left the Thunder and signed with the Warriors as a free agent, a move that didn't go over well in Oklahoma. It did go over well in the San Francisco Bay area, however, as the Warriors rode their newest star—and their collection of holdover stars—throughout the 2016–17 season of redemption, which ended in their defeating the Cavaliers to capture the NBA title.

Durant scored 30 or more points in each of the five games against the Cavs. In one of the most dominating performances in finals history, he averaged 35.4 points, 8.2 rebounds, and 5.4 assists and was named MVP.

After the championship-clinching win, Durant took the opportunity to spread his thanks four ways.

First, he thanked his teammates: Steph Curry, Klay Thompson, Draymond Green, and others who had welcomed him to a team that had won a title two years earlier and still had plenty of offensive weapons. Adding Durant meant fewer touches of the ball for each of them. Yet they all placed winning above personal statistics.

"We did it together, man," Durant told the media in the postgame press conference. "They call us a super team, but there's been a lot of super teams that haven't worked. We came together and continued to believe in each other. We sacrificed, and we're champs now."

Next, Durant gave credit to a few people none of the assembled press were familiar with.

"People just continued to pour into me every single day," Durant said. "People like John Gray, Carl Lentz, and Adam Harrington. People you may never have heard of who poured into me every single day. I'm working every day, grinding, and believing in myself to make this happen, and to do it feels great."

Durant was referring to Pastor John Gray of Lakewood Church in Houston, Durant's hometown, and Pastor Carl Lentz of Hillsong Church in New York. Durant, who was raised without a father, wanted to thank the men who had filled a role as mentors and spiritual advisors and helped him grow in his faith. It was his faith, after all, that Durant said had grounded him in the over-the-top life of an NBA star.

"I read my Bible now all the time," Durant told *Athletes in Action*. "The Bible both pumps me up and balances me to play my best, but it also tells me more about the Lord and how I can live for Him and what all He has done for me. I'm not perfect by any means. I have a long way to go to become close to the Lord, but hopefully I can continue to stay on that path. I just want to grow spiritually with the Lord and get to know Him as well as I can. I'm keepin' strong at it, just tryin' to make my walk of faith a little better. That's making me a better person, opening my eyes to things, and I'm maturing. Feels good!

"In the Bible, [it says] the Lord exalts humility, and that's one thing I try to be all the time. When I'm talking in front of people or when people tell me I'm great, I [remind myself that I] can always be better. Humility comes before honor. I always work on what I have now. I have to be thankful to the Lord for the gifts He's given me. My gift back to Him is to always be humble and always work as hard as I can."[1]

Durant next thanked the Golden State fans. A week after the victory, he took out a full-page ad in the *San Francisco Chronicle* to thank the fans for embracing and welcoming him. It was especially meaningful after the way OKC fans reacted to his leaving. The message signed by Durant read:

> Thank you, everyone, for making my initial season with the Warriors an incredible and exhilarating championship experience.
>
> Great accomplishments are never achieved alone and are best when shared with others.
>
> KD

At the ensuing championship parade in the city, Durant shared similar thoughts with the Golden State fans.

"We have so much joy when we're out there on the court," Durant told them. "It means the world to me to win a championship for you guys, and hopefully we keep it going…Thanks a lot for your support."

Finally, Durant thanked the one human being who had been most responsible for him reaching the heights he has: his mother, Wanda Pratt.

Durant's mother was the stabilizing force in his life through a challenging childhood. When Durant was an infant, his father deserted the family. Wanda and Durant's grandmother raised him.

Wanda sacrificed her own career goals, working long hours to make sure Durant and his brother had a solid home life and opportunity and that they felt loved.

So it was fitting that, after the final game, Durant made his way through the mass of reporters, players, coaches, and league officials swarming the court to find his mom.

He threw his arms around her. Locked in an embrace at half-court, Wanda whispered into his ear, "No matter what anybody says, you did it. I'm proud of you, son."

Asked moments later what it meant for him to share the moment with his mother, Durant became emotional.

"She's seen me as a kid putting in [the] work," he told the press. "She's seen how I come home after losses and how tough I take it…it feels good to see it come full circle."

Later, when he accepted the NBA Finals MVP Award, Durant again singled out his mom.

"We did it," he said. "I told you when I was eight years old. We did it."

It was not the first time Durant had publicly thanked his mother for her sacrifice. When he accepted the NBA MVP Award in 2014 when he was with Oklahoma City, Durant spoke from the podium about his mother.

"The odds were stacked against us, a single parent with two boys by the time you were 21 years old," Durant said to Wanda. "You made us believe, kept us off the street, put clothes on our backs, food on the table. When you didn't eat, you made sure we ate. You went to sleep hungry. You sacrificed for us…You're the real MVP."

It was a true Hollywood moment. Two years later, a movie was produced about Wanda's story for the Lifetime Network. It was titled—you guessed it—*The Real MVP: The Wanda Durant Story*.

That is the Durant story: mother and son—both MVPs.

"Many days I kinda pinch myself and say that any day this can all be gone," Durant said. "I know if I start to get a big head, my mom and others are going to do a great job of bringing me back down to size. I have the best support system with God above and His Word within me as well as a great team of coaches, family, friends, and mentors all circling me. I'm in pretty good hands. I believe!"

In talking after his mother's example, Durant has started a foundation to help kids who face similar situations as he did growing up. He says he feels this is the most important part of his legacy.

"I want to be known for serving people," Durant told an audience at Life.Church. "When people see me, they think I deserve something. I don't deserve anything. I don't deserve to be put in the front of the line at the movies or get a free meal. I don't deserve anything. I think for me, I just wanna go up to people and impact their lives. Whether it's from me inspiring them from playing basketball or just going up and asking them how their family is doing, that's what I want to be known as.

"Also, a legacy changer. I didn't grow up with my dad in the household, and one of my main goals in life is to become a great dad, somebody their kids can wake up to every day and be a great husband. So hopefully I can accomplish those goals."[2]

JEREMY LIN

You may never have heard of Linsanity.

It is not a dangerous infectious disease, although it certainly proved to be infectious.

It's not even a disease, although it has spread—at times very quickly.

It has, however, caused some of those who have contracted it to temporarily lose their minds.

If you have heard of Linsanity, you are likely a rabid NBA fan. Because Linsanity is the phenomenon that occurred when the sensation that is Jeremy Lin started lighting up the NBA.

The most improbable story in recent NBA history played out before the nation when Lin broke into the NBA, smack-dab in the middle of the media capital of the world.

The New York Knicks, a franchise desperate for some magic, found some.

Lin, a point guard who seemingly came out of nowhere, created a momentary Elvis-like craze during an otherworldly stretch of games where he was part Michael Jordan, part Jackie Robinson, part Beatles.

In 2012 the Knicks, while in the midst of one of a string of disappointing seasons, took a gamble on the backup point guard and put him on the court. The result was astounding. Lin scored more points in his first five NBA starts than any other player in the modern era, and he created a public frenzy in the process.

It all stemmed from Lin's improbable story. After leading his high school team to the California state championship, Lin was not offered a Division-I scholarship—the only California Division II Player of the Year ever to not receive a scholarship. He ended up at Harvard, where he became a two-time All–Ivy League selection. Still, he went undrafted by the NBA in 2010. He was offered a summer contract with Dallas and then signed with Golden State. He rarely played and was assigned to the D League (Developmental League; now known as the G League) three times, where he toiled for the Reno Bighorns and Erie BayHawks (now the Lakeland Magic). Lin was eventually waived by the Warriors and the Houston Rockets before joining the Knicks for the 2011–12 season.

After joining the Knicks, he slept on a couch in his brother's one-bedroom apartment in New York. He later slept on the couch of team-mate Landry Fields because he didn't know if he would have a job or enough money for rent. Lin was a Harvard honors grad and an NBA player, and he was living like a basketball vagabond.

Until one fateful night in 2012.

Prior to February 4, 2012, Lin had played in just nine games for the Knicks, and he had averaged a pedestrian 6.1 minutes and 3.6 points per game. That night, with the Knicks needing a spark, they brought Lin off the bench early in a game against the New Jersey Nets. He poured in 25 points to go along with 5 rebounds and 7 assists to lead New York to a win, and the birth pangs of Linsanity began.

The next game Lin had 28 points and 8 assists in another Knicks win. Then it was 23 and 10 in a win over Washington. A couple of nights later he torched the Los Angeles Lakers for 38 points and 7 assists. Linsanity was now a full-blown hysteria.

After the game, Lakers star Kobe Bryant told the media, "Players playing that well don't usually come out of nowhere. It seems like they come out of nowhere, but if you go back and take a look, his skill level was probably there from the beginning. It probably just went unnoticed."[1]

Why Lin went unnoticed has been the source of much speculation over the years. He was tall enough at six-feet-three, although he was slight.

He handled the ball well but had not yet refined his jump shot. He was smart (a 4.2 GPA at Harvard) and had performed very well on the court at every level of play. Many have postulated that the reason for the oversight was Lin's heritage. He is Asian American. Only five other players who were part Asian had ever played in the NBA, and all of them with little success or fanfare. Lin is the first American of Chinese or Taiwanese descent ever to play in the league. Whether or not racism was a factor, Lin was showing everyone he belonged in the league. Which is something those in the D League saw, recognizing that he was grounded, smart, and savvy—more so than most his age.

"I am not really too worried about proving anything to anybody," Lin said.

The night after the Lakers win, Lin scored 20 points and had 8 assists in a win over Minnesota, and he was named the Eastern Conference Player of the Week after averaging 27.3 points, 8.3 assists, and 2.0 steals in his four starts. Three days later, Lin drained a game-winning three-pointer with less than a second remaining to defeat Toronto. He became the first NBA player to score at least 20 points and have 7 assists in each of his first five starts; his 136 points in those games bested Shaquille O'Neal's record of 129 over the same span. In the next game against Sacramento, Lin dished out 13 assists in another win. The Knicks were 7-0 with Lin in the lineup, and he was averaging a historic 24.4 points and 9.2 assists during the run. Inside New York's Madison Square Garden, fans chanted "M-V-P, M-V-P." People stayed in their seats, screaming, yelling, and snapping photos.

Lin's popularity was so intense that online sales of his jersey became the highest in the NBA and so broad that his popularity reached to China, where they voted him first in an online fan vote for his performance in the Rising Stars Challenge, despite only scoring two points.

It was the ultimate underdog story, and people from all over the world were eating it up—literally.

Boston-based Ben & Jerry's released a "Taste the Lin-Sanity" ice cream flavor, and Nike released a Jeremy Lin shoe.

The *New York Times* called Lin "the Knicks most popular player in a decade."[2]

He appeared on the cover of *Sports Illustrated* twice in a row—the third NBA player to do so. He also made the cover of *Time* in Asia. After this,

Forbes magazine wrote, "Congratulations, Jeremy. You have now made the cover of *Time* the same number of times as Michael Jordan."[3]

Within three weeks of his first game as a starter, at least seven e-books were being published on Lin, and the Global Language Monitor declared that *Linsanity* had met its criteria to be considered an English-language word. New York City restaurants introduced new food and bar items in honor of Lin. An airline advertised "Linsanely low prices," bids for his rookie trading card exceeded $21,000 on eBay, and the press circulated rumors—denied by Lin—that he was dating Kim Kardashian.

A documentary film about Lin, titled *Linsanity*, premiered in 2013 at the Sundance Film Festival. It was shown at numerous film festivals before making its way into art houses.

"I haven't done a computation, but it's fair to say that no player has created the interest and the frenzy in this short period of time, in any sport, that I'm aware of like Jeremy Lin has," said NBA commissioner David Stern.[4]

Despite Lin's sudden fame, former Sacramento Kings coach Keith Smart said, "I knew [Lin] before he was Linmania. He's still the same humble guy. The guy has not changed a bit, which is real special for a young man."

"A great story," Bryant said. "It's a testament to perseverance and hard work. A good example for kids everywhere."[5]

As the craziness tapered off, Lin still had a career to run. He signed with Houston for $25 million in the post-Linsanity off-season. He bounced from there to the Lakers, then to Charlotte, and then to Brooklyn in 2017 with the team against which his historic run began five years earlier.

Make no mistake, the following is still large. It's just not as all-encompassing as it once was.

"I think I've grown to embrace it and be a little more accustomed to it," Lin said. "I'm learning how to use that in the right way."

In Brooklyn, during the first game of the season, Lin suffered a torn patellar tendon, sidelining him for the rest of the 2017–18 season. Lin's experience had come full circle from adversity to unprecedented fame and back to adversity again. Still, he was undaunted.

"I've had a roller coaster of emotions that have ranged from determination to discouragement to optimism to defeat to anger to confusion," he wrote in an email to his fans. "I'm hoping to be joyful and grateful in the rehab process."

The fact that Lin's popularity has not inflated his ego is a testament to his self-awareness and the grounding he finds in his faith. He is described by those who best know him as possessing genuine desire, work ethic, and humility.

"I've surrendered that to God. I'm not in a battle with what everybody else thinks anymore," said Lin.

Rather than using his fame to develop a marketing product or a money machine when his career is over, Lin says he hopes to become a pastor who can lead nonprofit organizations, and he has talked of working in inner-city communities to help underprivileged children. He already has made a donation of $1,000,000 to Harvard.

For Lin, the miraculous events that began in 2012 are all about staying in an attitude of thankfulness.

"For me, it's just where God calls me to be, and as long as I know that, I will have peace deep down inside even though I might not enjoy what's going on or not enjoy what just happened," he said. "As long as I know I'm where God wants me to be, that's the most important thing. In my life He has taken me to a lot of different places and a lot of unexpected turns, but at the end, He's been faithful through it all."

> *"I'm not concerned with your liking me or disliking me...
> All I ask is that you respect me as a human being."*
>
> **JACKIE ROBINSON**

SIMONE MANUEL

It is common for Olympic athletes to feel the pride of carrying the hopes of their nation with them into competition.

It is, however, uncommon for an athlete to carry the hopes of an entire race.

Such was the case with Simone Manuel at the 2016 Summer Olympic Games in Rio. When she touched the wall to win the gold in a thrilling 100-meter freestyle race, she became the first African American woman ever to win an individual medal in Olympic swimming.

"All I can say is all glory to God," said Manuel in an interview with NBC as she fought back tears after the race. "It's definitely been a long journey these past four years. I'm just so blessed to have a gold medal... I'm just so blessed."

Manuel lagged behind the leaders for the first 50 meters of the race but staged a fierce comeback, passing several swimmers and catching Canada's Penny Oleksiak at the wall. They finished in a dead heat for gold.

"I was like, 'Oh, I'm on the medal stand,'" Manuel said. "And then I turned around and saw the 1 by my name, and I was super surprised.

"My first gold medal at my first Olympics is kind of a surprise to me,"

Manuel told reporters. "I never thought I would be in this position, but I'm so blessed and honored to be on the medal stand."

Manuel became the first American to win gold in the event since 1984. Her time of 52.7 set a new Olympic record and a new American record.

More than that, it lifted the weight of 104 years of history from Manuel's broad shoulders.

"Coming into the race, I tried to take weight of the black community off my shoulders. It's something I carry with me," she said. "But I do hope that it kind of goes away…The title 'black swimmer' makes it seem like I'm not supposed to be able to win a gold medal or I'm not supposed to break records. And that's not true…I train hard and want to win just like everyone else."

She tried to hold back tears, but she couldn't. The tears weren't just for her pursuit or accomplishment. Rather she thought about the platform the win would give her and how she would forever be remembered. Manuel showed she clearly belonged with the best in the world, regardless of color. After preparation that took nearly a lifetime, she became a role model in less than a minute.

"This medal is not just for me," Manuel said. "It's for a whole bunch of people who came before me and have been an inspiration for me…This medal is for the people who come behind me and get into the sport and hopefully find love and drive to get to this point…I just want to be an inspiration to others that you can do it."

After the race, Manuel used her social media platforms to express more of her emotion and gratitude.

She tweeted, "It is an honor to represent the USA! God is working in me! I am so blessed and grateful. Thanks, you all, so much for your support."

In another post she tweeted: "All Glory to God! Isn't He awesome! I am extremely blessed."

Manuel's performance was not only historic, it was stunning. The field included the world record holder and holders of the other two top fastest times in the world. The then 20-year-old from Sugar Land, Texas, hadn't arrived in Rio expecting to win gold.

"It means a lot, especially with what's going on in the world today, just with some of the issues with police brutality," Manuel said. "This win kind of helps bring hope and change to some of the issues that are going on in the world. I went out there and swam as fast as I could, and my color just comes with the territory."

Manuel grew up in Texas. Her parents put her in swim lessons at age four so she'd learn how to be safe in water. She enjoyed it so much, she became a competitive swimmer at age nine.

She often struggled with being African American in a sport typically dominated by white athletes.

"I see other blacks and African Americans doing basketball, and running and doing volleyball, so I think the hardest part was coming to terms with, you know, this is what you love to do, so you should do it," she told CNN.[1]

During her senior year in high school, she broke the national record in the 50-meter freestyle for her age group.

Her competitiveness was instilled, in large part, by her family. Her two older brothers and her father all played college basketball. There were many competitions at home where Simone mixed it up with her brothers.

"I am fortunate that I have two older brothers, and they have definitely helped me with being competitive just to keep up with them," she told *USA Swimming.* "We were always encouraged to try what we wanted to do. As long as we tried our hardest and did the best we could, it didn't matter what we did."[2]

As part of that freedom, Manuel decided to leave Texas and head to Stanford for college. She selected the school for what it represents.

"You have to work hard and be pretty smart to get into a school like this—but honestly, that's another reason why I picked it, because I wanted to be in this atmosphere and challenge myself," she told *USA Swimming.*[3]

Her Stanford team included Olympic gold medalists Katie Ledecky and Maya DiRado. Talk about tough opponents.

All of it prepared Manuel to handle things in Rio. Along with her historic win, she also teamed with Abbey Weitzeil, Dana Vollmer, and Ledecky to earn a silver medal and a new American record in the 4x100 relay, her first event. She then followed up her individual gold in the 100 with an individual silver medal in the 50-meter freestyle, finishing just two one-hundredths of a second behind the gold medal winner. In her final race, she swam the anchor leg of Team USA's gold medal win in the 4x100 medley relay to earn her fourth medal and second gold of the games.

The games were a coming out party of sorts for Manuel, who established herself as one of the top short distance swimmers in the world. She followed with an amazing performance at the 2017 World Championships.

She and her teammates won gold and set an American record in the 4x100 freestyle relay. Along with her teammates, she won gold and set a world record in the 4x100 mixed medley relay. She beat the world record holder by four one-hundredths of a second to win gold in the 100-meter freestyle. She won bronze in the 50-meter freestyle, becoming the first American woman to swim under 24 seconds in that race. She finished the event by teaming up again to take the gold and set a new world record in the 4x100 medley relay.

Manuel left the championships with quite a haul: four golds and a bronze to go with two world records and one American record.

Back at Stanford, she took home even more hardware at the 2017 NCAA Championships. She was part of the first-place 800-meter freestyle relay team. Then she took second in the 200-meter freestyle relay. She won the 50-meter freestyle, breaking the NCAA record. She then took two thirds: the 200-meter freestyle and the 200-meter medley relay. Manuel then became the first female to swim under 46 seconds in the 100-meter freestyle in winning that event, and then she led off the winning 400-meter freestyle relay. Stanford won the team title, and Manuel went home with seven medals—four first-place finishes, a second, and two thirds.

Her historic run has given Manuel's supporters hope that she can affect diversity in a sport in which only 1 percent of competitors are African American.

"I'm super glad with the fact that I can be an inspiration to others and hopefully diversify the sport," she told the assembled press afterward. "But at the same time, I would like there to be a day where there are more of us and it's not, 'Simone, the black swimmer.'"

"This is the first test of a gentleman: his respect for those who can be of no possible value to him."

WILLIAM LYON PHELPS

JORDAN SPIETH

> **»FACTOIDS**

His grandfather was an orchestra conductor.

He missed his high school graduation to play in the 2011 Byron Nelson Classic.

J ordan Spieth is human.

What a relief.

His final-round defeat at the Masters in 2016 was a huge letdown for the media, who had hoped he would be perfect. That performance had the media asking what was wrong with him and speculating as to the reason for his "collapse" at Augusta. Was he emotionally fragile? Was he distracted? Was he a victim of too much success too soon?

Nope. He's just imperfect. Fallible. Unable to win every week, rise to every occasion, make every shot. Human.

But for a human, he is pretty amazing.

Pop culture seems to demand our up-and-coming athletes be "the next Tiger, Michael, LeBron," you fill in the blank. No matter their accomplishments, we want them to be more. Perhaps our desire to elevate people to hero status or proclaim them as "the greatest" is due in part to the dichotomy that exists in our postmodern culture that minimizes the concept of God yet desperately seeks someone to worship.

Spieth is uncomfortable with the idea of being worshipped. He's actually quite humble, kind, and gracious. And he is *not* emotionally fragile.

It's likely Spieth silenced his critics when he made an improbable comeback to capture the British Open in 2017. It gave him the third leg of the career grand slam. He also joined Jack Nicklaus as the only golfers to have won three of the four major championships before turning 24. He did it with an ice-in-his-veins chip from an unplayable lie.

Down by one stroke to Matt Kuchar on the thirteenth hole of the final round, Spieth navigated his way out of the unplayable lie and bogeyed the hole. He then played the final five holes in five under par and beat Kuchar by two strokes. The questions about his emotional strength went away.

Spieth comes from an athletic family. His dad played baseball at Lehigh University. His mom played basketball at Moravian College. His younger brother, Steven, is a basketball player at Brown University. It was a hypercompetitive household.

"The first time Steven could beat Jordan at anything was chess, and the board got thrown," Spieth's mother, Chris, said. "He'll tell you today it's because Steven was in chess club—he was only in second grade."[1]

Spieth's first childhood love wasn't golf. He loved baseball and was an outstanding left-handed pitcher. Golf was almost accidental. He wanted to do something other than swimming lessons one summer and picked golf. At the age of 14 he put away his baseball glove to pursue golf full-time.

"The hardest part for me was quitting baseball," Spieth said. "I was starting high school, and my dad was a baseball player. So that was a tough one."

Tough choice, yes. Good choice, no doubt.

He won two U.S. Junior Amateur Championships—only the second player ever to win multiple juniors (Tiger Woods is the other)—and was an American Junior Golf Association first-team All-American three times.

As a high school junior, Spieth was invited to play in his first PGA Tour event, the HP Byron Nelson Championship. He was in contention for the first three rounds and ended up tying for sixteenth—as a 16-year-old.

"I realized I could at that time play on tour and compete with those guys," said Spieth.

"That's the week when he knew he was going to be a successful professional someday," his father said. "He knew that's what he wanted to do, but that week validated that not only was he going to do it, but he was going to have success at it."[2]

That performance thrust him into the national spotlight. As a junior, he was selected to the victorious 2011 Walker Cup team, where he had an undefeated record—as a 17-year-old.

Spieth went to the University of Texas, where he helped the Longhorns win the 2012 NCAA Team Championship in his freshman year and was named first-team All-American.

Spieth turned pro in 2013. He won his first tournament shortly thereafter, becoming the youngest PGA Tour winner in 82 years. He finished the season ranked seventh on the FedEx Cup and became the youngest ever to play in the Presidents Cup.

At the age of 20 he finished second at the Masters and played on the U.S. Ryder Cup team.

In 2015 Spieth put together what is considered as one of the most historic golf seasons with 5 victories and 15 total top-ten finishes. He shattered records with his first major victory at the Masters, setting marks for the lowest 36-hole and 54-hole scoring records, most birdies (26) in 72 rounds, and tying the 72-hole scoring record. He is the second youngest to win the Masters, behind only Tiger Woods. Later that year he won the U.S. Open Championship, becoming the youngest golfer ever to hold the first two legs of golf's four majors, at just 21-years old, and only the fifth to achieve it (joining Ben Hogan, Arnold Palmer, Jack Nicklaus, and Tiger Woods).

He finished the season as the number-one ranked player in the world and was unanimously voted the Player of the Year. He won a record $23 million that year. That is when the hysteria surrounding him blew up.

"The last time we had a child like this, there were three wise men and a donkey involved," said golf analyst David Feherty.[3]

"First, first, fourth, second—just astonishing in this day and age," Feherty continued. "One shot away from the playoff in the British, and as close as he came at the PGA, one of the great seasons in professional golf history. No sign of slowing down, either. He expected that of himself each week that he teed it up. That's what great players do. They expect to play well every week, and they're shocked when they don't."

"If I could somehow duplicate that year for the rest of my career, I would be pretty pleased," Spieth said.

He didn't quite duplicate that success in 2016, but he still won two tournaments. In 2017 he won three, including the Open, which gave him 11 career Tour victories before turning 24.

"He can be great," said Tiger Woods. "A rare talent," Phil Mickelson agreed. "A superstar," said Paul Azinger. "A special young kid," said Jack Nicklaus.[4]

He truly is special. The fruit of Spieth's faith can be seen in the way he conducts himself on and off the green, not the least of which is his impressive humility. Self-aware and with a desire to serve others and put their needs above his own, he is a unique superstar whose world does not revolve around himself. In fact, if anything, his world revolves around his younger sister.

"We say all the time—our friends and his friends—we all live in Ellie's world," said Spieth's mother. "No matter what's going on, it's all about her. At least she thinks that."[5]

Ellie was born prematurely with a still undiagnosed neurological disorder that left her developmentally challenged. As a *New York Times* story reported, Ellie's life is "a happy dance interrupted by cloudbursts."[6]

"She's the most special part of our family," Spieth said. "She's the funniest part of our family."

"I love spending time with her. It's humbling to see the struggles she goes through each day that we take for granted. Because of Ellie, it has always been a priority to me to be in tune to the needs of others."

Inspired by Ellie, Spieth fulfilled a lifelong dream by launching the Jordan Spieth Family Foundation. The focus of the charity is to provide financial assistance and a platform for supporting children with special needs, military families, junior golf programs, and pediatric cancer.

At the age of 19, Spieth recognized the opportunity his sudden platform provided. He dreamed of building a philanthropic legacy as large as an athletic one. Now, he is building his most important legacy, with hopes to one day be the most charitable athlete foundation.

"With Ellie and how we grew up with her and her struggles and her triumphs, I think it just put life a little more in perspective than maybe it would have had we not experienced it," Spieth said. "My parents are such great parents that I don't think it would have changed much, but we were able to see firsthand what someone who struggles like that is like, and it certainly took over our family. So maybe that's what helps keep me 'normal.' I don't know what the alternative is when everyone says maturity and grounded."

Spieth can't fathom what his life would be like without Ellie and how it would have affected his personality.

"I don't know what the alternative would be," he said. "Would I be a brat?"

During his senior year in high school, Spieth spent one day a week volunteering at Ellie's school. It made their bond deeper. Spieth expressed so in a tribute he wrote in the school yearbook.

"Ellie, I know every day presents its fair share of struggles, but the fight that you show every day inspires everyone who knows you," he wrote. "Spending each Wednesday with you this year has been a blessing, and I love you."

"Integrity is not a conditional word. It doesn't blow in the wind or change with the weather. It is your inner image of yourself, and if you look in there and see a man who won't cheat, then you know he never will."

—JOHN D. MACDONALD

principle
virtue goodness

INTEGRITY

honorableness
righteousness honesty
stability sincerity
purity wholeness
coherence

"There is no pillow so soft as a clear conscience."

FRENCH PROVERB

MARCUS MARIOTA

> **»FACTOIDS**

His parents originally did not want him to play tackle football.

He has built homes in Nashville with Habitat for Humanity.

The Hawaiian Islands have not traditionally been thought of as a hotbed for NFL talent. In the history of the league, just over 100 players from Hawaii have graced NFL team rosters. Only three of them became All Pros, and just six made it to a Pro Bowl.

But Tennessee Titans quarterback Marcus Mariota just might be changing that.

In 2012 the Honolulu native's breakout performance as a redshirt freshman at the University of Oregon altered the football landscape in Hawaii. It was the beginning of a career that has included college football records, the Heisman Trophy, a place as the second pick in the NFL draft, NFL rookie records, and a reputation as one of the best young quarterbacks in the game.

Mariota's success on the field and his character and humility off have inspired young athletes in Hawaii to forego surfing and baseball and follow in his footsteps. Case in point: The nation's top-ranked high school quarterback recruit in 2017 was Tua Tagovailoa, who ended up leading Alabama to the national championship as a true freshman. Tagovailoa watched on television in 2014 as Mariota became the first Hawaii-born athlete and first Polynesian to receive the Heisman Trophy. Tagovailoa carefully took in Mariota's words from the podium that night.

"To the Polynesian community, I hope and pray that this is only the beginning," Mariota said while clutching the Heisman. "Young Poly athletes everywhere, you should take this as motivation, and dream big and strive for greatness."

Tagovailoa's dreams were birthed that night. He followed in Mariota's footsteps at Honolulu St. Louis High School. Mariota tutored him for years in both the game and in the development of his character. Now Tagovailoa is taking a similar path to success.

"Marcus showed me that kids like us can win the Heisman," Tagovailoa told *Sports Illustrated*. "That we can compete with kids from the mainland."[1]

Dreams were birthed in numerous other Hawaiian youth that night as well, as the number of kids attending quarterback camps on the islands has exploded since then.

It is a remarkable example of how one man can inspire a state and its people and build a pathway for others to follow.

It seems Mariota has always been dedicated to being an example for others.

At Oregon he passed for more than 10,000 yards and 105 touchdowns while rushing for more than 2,000 yards and 29 more scores. He set five Pac-12 records and six school records. He was a first-team All-American and took home the Walter Camp, Johnny Unitas, Davey O'Brien, Maxwell, and Manning awards. He also graduated with a general science degree the same month he won the Heisman.

But more than his performance on the field, those around him have consistently lauded Mariota the human being.

"We try to find something wrong with him," Sione Thompson, the assistant principal at St. Louis High, told *Sports Illustrated*.[2]

Mariota was such an upstanding citizen that the biggest concern among NFL scouts before the draft was that he might be *too* nice, *too* polite.

I'm sure his parents were mortified to learn that.

Nice became *nice* throw, *nice* read, and *nice* run as Mariota was spectacular in his NFL debut. Playing against Tampa Bay and the quarterback drafted ahead of him (Jameis Winston), Mariota had the best first-game passing performance in NFL history. He completed 13 of 15 passes for

209 yards and four touchdowns. He became the first quarterback in history with a perfect passer rating of 158.3 in his first regular-season game and the first quarterback in history to throw four touchdown passes in the first half of his NFL debut. *Nice* start!

At six-feet-four, 222 pounds, Mariota has prototypical NFL quarterback size. However, he has speed and elusiveness few other quarterbacks in the league have. The combination, along with a high level of intelligence, make him a budding star.

In 2017 he led the Titans to their first playoff berth since 2008, passing for more than 3,200 yards on the season. The Titans upset the Kansas City Chiefs in the first round of the AFC playoffs before losing to the New England Patriots in the second round. In the win over Kansas City, Mariota became the first player in NFL history to throw a touchdown pass and catch a touchdown pass. And it happened on the same play. It was one of the strangest plays in memory.

Mariota lined the Titans up for a third-and-goal from the Chiefs six-yard line. His pass was deflected by Darrelle Revis right back into Mariota's hands. Mariota snagged the ball and dove into the end zone, making it the first time a quarterback had thrown a touchdown pass to himself in the postseason.

Mariota, the guy who drives his teammates around in the off-season so they can drink beer but says he's never had a sip of it, and who often takes the blame for a mistake by someone else even when it's not true, has gained the respect and admiration of his teammates.

"He can run, he can pass, he can block," Titans running back Derrick Henry told *The Sporting News*. "You ever seen *Friday Night Lights*? He can do it all."[3]

"Marcus is our leader in the huddle," center Ben Jones told the *Memphis Daily News*. "He's a guy who you can count on at all times. He's the most focused guy. He's the calmest guy always, and he's a competitor. I wouldn't want anybody else in the huddle with me."[4]

"It's pretty awesome, especially as mild mannered as he is," tackle Taylor Lewan told the *Bend Bulletin*. "His competitive nature is bigger than anybody else's in here, so I know he wants to win every single game, and we're just here to help him do that."[5]

"Good things happen to positive people, and Marcus is the most positive person I've ever been around," said receiver Rishard Matthews. "It just shows. He's going to be at the ball, trying to make a play, whether the ball is in his hands or he's trying to make a lead block…That's what you want from a leader."[6]

His calm leadership comes from Mariota's center, which is his faith.

"Football doesn't define me. It's just what I do," Mariota told *FCA Magazine*. "That was a huge life lesson for me. I really took that and ran with it. My faith is what keeps me going, and I can always grow in that.

"God has taught me that I can trust in Him. No matter what—whether things are good or bad—I know I can always trust in Him. And that has really allowed me to go 'all in' for Him.

"As an athlete, when you're able to go out there and have the abilities that the Lord has blessed you with, you want to…go out there to represent Him in the right light. To represent your family in the right light, and to do that through His power."[7]

MAYA MOORE

»FACTOIDS

ESPN Sports Science determined that Moore's hand speed is faster than the strike of a rattlesnake.

She was named to Forbes 30 Under 30: The Sports World's Brightest Young Stars for 2015.

Maya Moore is one of the most recognizable faces in all of women's sports. The Minnesota Lynx star forward was named *Sports Illustrated*'s Performer of the Year in 2017 after capturing her fourth WNBA championship.

In fact, it seems that all Moore does is win.

At every stage of her sport, that's all she has done. In high school, she won three state titles at Collins Hill High in Georgia. She then captured two NCAA titles at the University of Connecticut, and with the Lynx, she has won four titles in seven seasons.

Moore was selected number one overall by the Lynx in the 2011 WNBA Draft. Since then, along with her four championships, she has been named a WNBA All-Star five times and was the 2013 WNBA Finals MVP, selected as the WNBA All-Star Game MVP twice, and won the 2011 WNBA Rookie of the Year.

Media, experts, and fans alike are all predicting Moore is on her way to becoming the league's all-time greatest player. Due to her dynamic play and sterling character, she was sought out by Michael Jordan to become the Jordan brand's first female basketball signee.

With all her accomplishments—both team and personal—Moore is not at a loss for motivation.

"There are a lot of things I'm motivated by," Moore told ESPN. "I think number one, it just comes down to being at a place where I know I've been given a great gift. I feel like God has blessed me with so many opportunities and talents and different people in my life. I just want to say thank you and live my life and compete in a way where I'm putting it all out there in everything that I do, that I'm an example.

"I've been given a platform. I've been given an opportunity to be an example and a shining light to bring people joy through sports. That's really fun for me. That's really satisfying. I love to compete. I love to play ball."

In 2017 that love of the game brought the Lynx back from the brink in the finals. Down 2-1 to the Los Angeles Sparks, it was Moore who pulled the lynx back, turning Game 4 around and then dropping in 18 points and pulling down 10 rebounds to give the Lynx an 85–76 win and the championship. It was a typical Moore performance, coming up big in the biggest games.

So what more can Moore do for a Maya Moore encore? Win more perhaps. She remains driven to be the best, a drive that is somewhat fed by her upbringing.

Moore shares a strong bond with her mother, Kathryn Moore, as an only child. As a single mother, Kathryn saw unlimited potential in Maya and was determined to help her go as far as possible in life. She taught Maya to dream.

"We had no idea that I'd be where I am today," Moore said. "She [Mom] was just hoping I'd be five-feet-nine and make it to college."

For the first 11 years of her life, Moore was surrounded by loving extended family members in Jefferson City, Missouri. They helped make up for the absence of Maya's biological father. Kathryn's career eventually took her and Maya to Charlotte, North Carolina, and then Suwanee, Georgia. By the time she was in eighth grade, Maya had attended four different middle schools.

Maya sought stability and found it in her faith—the one constant amid all the moving boxes and new desks.

"When my mom got laid off from the job for which we had moved and then had to work nights for a while, that produced the perfect storm for us to have to depend on the guidance and stability God provided," she recalled. "I began to see God as my Father."

This was no small step for her, considering she had never known a father.

"That was a vivid part for me in finding security and peace in knowing who I was because I knew who He was and because He relates to each of us as a Father," she said. "It was a really powerful way for me to understand and relate to God."

That peace fueled Moore's emotional maturity, which coincided with her physical growth. By her senior year in high school, Moore was the nation's top recruit, having won back-to-back Naismith National High School Player of the Year awards. During her four years, her high school team posted a 125-3 record and in 2007 was given the *USA Today* mythical national championship.

At UConn, her teams went 150-4 and appeared at the Final Four at the conclusion of all four seasons. Moore won three consecutive State Farm Wade Trophy National Player of the Year honors (2009–11).

During her first season in Minneapolis, the Lynx were transformed from a 13-21 team in 2010 to league champions in 2011 with a 29-7 record.

To commemorate its twentieth anniversary, the WNBA selected a 20@20 list in 2016. It was a list of the league's 20 all-time greatest players, selected by a special panel. At the age of 27, Moore was the youngest player on the roster.

Want more winning? How about Moore's two Olympic gold medals in 2012 and 2016. For her basketball career—from high school to the WNBA—her team's winning percentage is over .850.

"We couldn't have timed it better than He [God] did," Maya told Athletes in Action. "All those amazing teams I played for, keeping me healthy—I know it's His provision blessing my life and my family. I've also tried to work as hard as I can, taking the gifts He's given me and living fully in it all. I've tried to be an example of someone with a great work ethic who enjoys the journey at the same time."[1]

Yet for all the winning, Moore is not a household name. And she likes it that way. Moore is not interested in the fame that some athletes crave. She gets more excited about impacting other people's lives. She has thrown her time and energy behind various social causes, with a focus on those most underserved.

For example, she took up the cause of 16-year-old Jonathan Irons, a small-time drug dealer sentenced to 65 years in prison in 1998, which was related to a shooting that occurred the previous year in Missouri.

Irons had pleaded not guilty to the charges, claiming he had been seen at a friend's house a few blocks away when the crime occurred and finger-prints at the crime scene did not match his.

Moore learned about the case when she was nine. As Moore researched the case, she became a voice for Irons. She even occasionally joined her family members on regular trips to prison to visit him. She ended up becoming one of Irons's biggest advocates, working for his exoneration.

Since her childhood, Moore has been passionate about helping those who are marginalized. While other athletes' role models are typically those who have gone before them in their sport, Moore's childhood hero was Coretta Scott King because of the change she helped create. For Moore, life is about reform.

"We are to be Christ's hands and feet," she said. "We're called to be loving neighbors. It might not be as popular, but we have to give a voice to the voiceless."

"She is so passionate," said Lynx chaplain Michelle Backes. "She can hardly contain it in a game—in a good way—and I think that's how it is inside her [spiritually], as well. When she sees injustice of any kind, I think that strikes a chord."

Moore also pours her passion into efforts to end human trafficking and slavery through the End It movement.

"Turning a blind eye to injustice," she told *Sharing the Victory* maga-zine, "is the opposite of what the Bible says."[2]

Winning off the court with large-scale social issues such as these are paramount for Moore. She is dedicated to using her platform to make a difference where it truly matters.

"Faith is at the core of who I am, everything that I do," Moore told *Sports Spectrum* magazine. "I think God has created me in a way that I have certain talents, I have certain gifts, and I have certain passions, and the more I try to develop those and live them out, I feel like I'm fulfill-ing my purpose. It's bigger than just scoring a basket; it's the impact I can make on somebody.

"I feel like I found purpose. When you find your purpose and you find what you're supposed to do, it's a beautiful thing."[3]

"The truth is not always the same as the majority decision."

POPE JOHN PAUL II

BENJAMIN WATSON

The ongoing mantra in football is that the letters NFL stand for "Not for Long," indicating the brevity of a career in the league. The average NFL career spans 3.3 years. It is an industry that constantly seeks younger and fresher talent while injury and/or the effect of a repeated number of hits often sends men home early.

It is rare to see a player last in the league beyond a decade. Rarer still if that player is not a quarterback or kicker.

So it seems that Benjamin Watson is a rare athlete. To last 14 seasons at the physical position of tight end is uncommon.

Over his career, Watson has hauled in 495 passes for over 5,400 yards and 42 touchdowns. He's been part of a Super Bowl championship and has caught passes from two of the most prolific quarterbacks in NFL history: Tom Brady and Drew Brees.

The sustained success is a testament to Watson's approach to the game.

"My desire is to honor God with the talents He's given me. That means dedicating myself to being the best I can be at my craft," Watson told *Sports Spectrum* magazine.[1]

Rarer still, at least in the public purview, Watson is a man of intellect. He scored a 48 on the Wonderlic test—the achievement test given to all draft-eligible college players. The score was one of the three highest in the history of the exam and is said to reflect an IQ of 142, which would place him in the ninety-ninth percentile of all people.

Even more rare, Watson is a man who has used his platform to thoughtfully speak out about key issues that affect American culture.

Watson was born and raised in Norfolk, Virginia, and his father, Ken, played linebacker for the University of Maryland while his mother, Diana, competed in synchronized swimming. Watson dreamed of following in his father's footsteps and playing college football.

His dream was realized after a high school career in South Carolina, where Watson became an all-state selection and was voted student of the year. Then, after three stellar seasons at the University of Georgia, Watson became the New England Patriots first-round draft choice in 2004.

As a rookie, Watson was on the injured list for almost the entire 2004 season. Still, he was part of the Patriots team that won Super Bowl XXXIX. Over the next five years he became an integral part of the Patriots offense, catching 20 touchdown passes during that span. With New England, he made four more trips to the postseason, scoring on a 63-yard catch and run against Jacksonville in 2005 and scoring twice in 2007. He was also part of the Patriots team that lost to the New York Giants in Super Bowl XLII.

In 2010, after signing a free-agent contract, Watson led the Cleveland Browns with 68 receptions, 763 receiving yards, and three receiving touchdowns. After three productive seasons in Cleveland, Watson moved on to New Orleans as a free agent in 2013, where he played with Brees. There, in 2015 and at the age of 35, he enjoyed his best season, catching 74 passes for 825 yards, and six touchdowns—all career highs. He was named a Saints team captain for the 2015 season.

In 2016 he joined the Baltimore Ravens as a free agent. He sat out the entire 2016 season after suffering a torn Achilles tendon in the team's third preseason game. Watson tweeted a message of thanks for the public support he received after the injury.

"And we know that in all things God works for the good of those who love him, who have been called according to his purpose" (Romans 8:28).

The time off for surgery, recovery, and rehab, while challenging, was profitable for Watson.

"The time spent with my family, writing, reading, rehabbing, speaking, wondering, crying, questioning, and trusting were all part of the good as well," he said. "And that 'good' will continue throughout our entire lives on this earth. It's football, and our bodies break. Yet God is not silent, and He will draw us closer to Him even in disappointment."

Downtime from the injury also provided opportunities to get closer to his father—now a pastor—and to invest himself in his own children.

"I spent a lot of time talking to my father," Watson said. "He is my biggest supporter and, outside of my wife, the person I talk to the most. He would check on me every week to see how I was feeling during my rehab. In my conversations with Daddy, he would remind me about God's faithfulness.

"Since I was home a bit more, it was important to be the father and husband I should be. There is always room for growth in this area!"

The experience inspired Watson to write his second book. *The New Dad's Playbook: Gearing Up for the Biggest Game of Your Life* was penned to help expectant fathers and support their wives who are having children.

"Men should be involved in their children's lives from conception to adulthood," Watson wrote about the book on his website. "For the moment, accept that there will be some things you just aren't good at—at least, not right away. Have you changed a diaper? Practice makes perfect."[2]

In the book Watson explains the pregnancy process, childbirth, and child-rearing with advice and very real and personal stories.

"This book is part exhortation and part instruction. Our first goal for this book was to practically prepare men to be the fathers, husbands, and supports their wives need them to be. The second is to encourage men to know they have what it takes to be a father. No matter what our background is or what our own father was like or not like, we are needed as fathers. We can become the fathers we want to be.

"What I've realized…is that you don't have to be perfect to be the perfect dad. Nor do you have to be the perfect husband. What you need is the willingness to admit when you're wrong and be willing to grow into the man you were created to be. Be open to change. Prepare for the relationship you want to have with the mother of your children. Prepare for the relationship you'll have with your children."[3]

Watson had started on the book a year earlier. When the injury necessitated his sitting out the season, he found he had enough time to complete it. He presented it as one imperfect father sharing with other imperfect fathers what he's learned after having five children.

"There's no perfect dad because there are no perfect people," Watson said. "It's never too late to make up for lost time. You can go forward. Your children need you...Even if you don't know what to do, you have what it takes. A man needs to know that he has what it takes...As men, we need to be willing to stand in the gap for those who don't have fathers too.

"I believe fathers are to be the protectors, providers, priests, and spiritual leaders within our families. Though we do this imperfectly, it's what we're called to do...As fathers, we have the chance to change generations by the way we lead our children. What kind of father are you going to be?"[4]

This was not the first time Watson had stirred hearts through his writing. His first book, *Under Our Skin: Getting Real About Race—And Getting Free from the Fears and Frustrations That Divide Us,* was released in 2015. It was birthed out of a Facebook post by Watson in late 2014 that went viral and changed his life.

After the events of August 2014 in Ferguson, Missouri, Watson wrote a Facebook post on the issue of race in America. In the post, he thoughtfully expressed a range of emotions—from his anger over injustice and frustration over a culture that glorifies altercation to his hopefulness that things are changing, and his encouragement that God is the answer.

The post was liked on Facebook more than 850,000 times and received national attention. Suddenly Watson was at the center of the race discussion in America, providing his perspective on Fox News, CNN, and other outlets. He has remained at the center since, being asked to comment on the NFL national anthem protests.

"It pains me to see people not stand and honor the flag during the anthem," Watson told CNN. "I believe every American should desire to stand for our anthem, but sometimes an American decides to use their agency to draw attention to an issue of concern. I support the players who decided to sit, because they are not doing so flippantly but because of a sincere conviction. It is their decision. There is more than one way to advocate and be a voice.

"There are some disgusting things that happen in this country and continue to happen in this country, not only in the past but also in the present. But it's still my homeland, it's still where my family lives, it's still where I was born, it's still the flag I will raise. And so, by default, I would say that we want to stand for our country until there's a time when we feel like we can't, and what I saw was a young man who decided that this was a time when he couldn't stand for the national anthem, and that was his way of protest…[Colin Kaepernick] wasn't violent. He exercised his rights and started a conversation—and for that I applaud him. However, if I were playing this year, I would be standing because for me, that's not my mode of protest."[5]

Watson believes the issues that plague the nation must be faced head-on, with people of faith opening their eyes to seeing the issues in a new way.

"We are in an awakening point. Inside, our hearts are still dealing and reeling over many of the same issues we've had throughout the history of this country," he said. "I'm going to stick to truth, but I want to do it in a way that speaks truth in love.

"The church has the illusion of togetherness and unity, but there is a large portion of the church that looks different and, many times, worse than their secular counterparts. The church should be leading the way when it comes to relationships between different ethnicities."

Watson's influence is compounded through the foundation he launched with his wife, Kirsten, to carry hope and God's love to those in the greatest of need: meeting physical and spiritual needs and battling sex trafficking, with the mission of always reaching "one more."

Ben came back from the Achilles injury to have a strong 2017 season, leading the Ravens with 61 catches for four scores.

His impact on and off the field has led to his recognition as one of CNN's Most Extraordinary People of the Year in 2014, the Saints 2015 NFL Walter Payton Man of the Year nominee, an NFLPA 2015 Byron "Whizzer" White Award nominee, a 2015 NFL Art Rooney Sportsmanship Award nominee, a Walter Payton Man of the Year finalist in 2016 and nominee in 2017, the Ravens' Ed Block Courage Award winner in 2017, and the Bart Starr Award recipient in 2018, honoring the NFL player who demonstrates outstanding character and leadership in the home, on the field, and in the community—all of which Watson believes are a reflection of his commitment to modeling the character of God.

"The number-one thing God has taught me and continues to teach me is that it is not about me" he said. "God has a plan that sometimes doesn't match up to my plan. But I put my faith and trust in Him that He has my best interest at heart and all things will work together for His glory...One of my favorite verses is Colossians 3:23: "Whatever you do, do it wholeheartedly as unto the Lord, not for men." Whether I'm playing football, being a husband to my wife, being a teammate, working out, studying, or being a parent, this verse challenges me to do it all to the glory of God."

"The challenge for all people of ambition is to recognize that the pursuit of success creates constant temptations to sacrifice integrity and that there is a point at which the price of success makes its fulfillment worthless."

MICHAEL S. JOSEPHSON

RUSSELL WILSON

He has two Great Danes named Amy and Prince.

There is a bus in Seattle named after him: "Bussell Wilson."

When NFL people talk about Russell Wilson, they don't focus on his success as a quarterback. In his first six years in the league, from 2012 to 2017, he has led the Seattle Seahawks to a 65-30 record—more wins in the first six years of a career than any other quarterback in NFL history—and to back-to-back Super Bowls, with one Super Bowl championship.

These same NFL wonks don't talk about his efficiency as a passer, even though he has thrown for more than 22,000 yards and 161 touchdowns during these six seasons, and he has thrown for more than 3,000 yards in every one of his NFL seasons.

They don't talk about his mobility, even though he has rushed for 3,275 yards in his career, including 849 yards in 2014, fifth all-time in single-season rushing yards for quarterback.

And they don't talk about his celebrity wife, Ciara. Well, okay. They might talk about her.

What they do talk about is the Seattle Seahawks quarterback's maturity.

Wilson has always seemed mature beyond his age, which likely comes from his upbringing.

Wilson was raised in a close-knit family in Richmond, Virginia. He spent most of his days playing sports with his older brother, Harry.

"Russell couldn't beat Harry, and he'd come inside and say, 'Mom, Harry's doing such and such,' and I'd say, 'Russell, if you can't handle it, then maybe you need to stay inside,'" his mom, Tammy, said. "He'd pout. 'No, no, no, I'm going back out there.' I think his brother really helped him to be tough because Harry wouldn't just let him win."

In the tenth grade Wilson beat out a six-foot-five eleventh grader to win the varsity quarterback job, a situation he would encounter again in college and in the NFL.

Wilson was profoundly influenced by his father, Harrison Wilson III, who went to Dartmouth and had a tryout with the San Diego Chargers before he became a lawyer. The elder Wilson instilled discipline and a work ethic in his son. He also instilled faith. Wilson's father died in 2010.

"My husband always told the boys if there's any kind of business situation, wear a suit and wear a tie," Tammy said. "That's why Russell is adamant about taking a shower and being well groomed after a game before he does his press conference."

Wilson's mother has long held to a specific Scripture for her son: 1 Samuel 16:7. "It's not the countenance of a man nor the height," she begins, "but the heart. The Lord does not look at the things people look at. People look at the outward appearance, but the Lord looks at the heart."

If anything epitomizes Wilson, it is this one truth. He will never allow his size to define him or stop him from achieving excellence. His mother also taught him not to be defined by what other people say.

Wilson has always been able to do things people said he couldn't. His unwavering belief has carried Wilson on his journey through two colleges and minor-league baseball to stardom in the NFL at a position some colleges said he was too short to play at five-feet-eleven.

He won three state championships in high school, but the university he wanted to play for—the University of Virginia—recruited a taller quarterback over Wilson.

So he went to North Carolina State, where he was the number-five quarterback on the depth chart at the beginning of fall camp and the starter in the season opener.

After passing for more than 8,500 yards and 76 touchdowns in three years with the Wolfpack, head coach Tom O'Brien was unhappy when Wilson wanted to skip spring practice before his senior season to play minor league baseball. Wilson, who had been drafted by the Colorado Rockies in the fourth round of the baseball draft, wanted to pursue both sports.

Since coach and player were at a standoff, Wilson decided to transfer. Because he had graduated in three years with a BA in communications, Wilson could go anywhere as a graduate transfer and play immediately. He chose Wisconsin, where he not only earned the starting job but had a historic season.

He led the Badgers to the Big 10 championship and a berth in the Rose Bowl. He passed for more than 3,000 yards with 33 touchdowns and just four interceptions. He set the single-season FBS record for passing efficiency at 191.8.

Even though he had the arm strength and the intangibles, Wilson was shorter than any quarterback in the NFL. Had he been six-feet-five, the scouts said, he would have been the number-one pick. As it turned out, the Seahawks picked him in the third round.

Wilson's father died the day after the draft and never got to see him throw an NFL pass.

Seattle head coach Pete Carroll, however, has seen plenty of them. It took three days of watching Wilson throw in minicamp for Carroll to see that Wilson deserved a shot at competing for the starting quarterback spot. After fall camp opened, it took three weeks for Carroll to determine Wilson would be the starter. Since then, he has become one of the most successful quarterbacks in the NFL.

"More than anything, I think they saw how I prepared," Wilson said. "I've been the same way throughout my whole life just by the way my parents raised me by focusing on the little details, the attention to detail."

Wilson's approach sets him apart. He studies relentlessly and believes in himself unwaveringly, and he has confidence. He refuses to be out-worked, outstudied, or outprepared. He has caused the sports world to stop looking at those few inches they say he lacks and instead see everything he does have.

Because of what they see in Wilson, he has become one of the most marketable players in the game. He has the biggest following on social media among all NFL players, with nearly 10 million fans combined on Facebook, Instagram, and Twitter. He also has off-field earnings of close to $10 million and endorsements with Alaska Airlines, Bose, Braun, Microsoft, Nike, Wilson, and more.

He's involved in several business ventures, recently founding TraceMe, a mobile-first platform to provide fans exclusive access to their favorite athletes, artists, and celebrities.

Speaking of celebrities, in 2016 Wilson and pop singer Ciara wed after a high-profile dating period in which they were mocked for practicing abstinence until their wedding night.

Wilson repeatedly said it was a demonstration of "the fact that we could love each other without that."

At the heart of such decisions for Wilson is his faith, which has given him a sense of priority and the maturity that has been evident for so long.

When Wilson's father died, he became a father figure for his younger sister, Anna. He gave her direction, instilled life principles and faith, and even sent her to basketball camp at Stanford, where she now plays for the nationally ranked women's basketball team. She prepares like her brother, competes like him, sees the world like him, and even talks like him, often repeating his maxims.

"It's like my dad always told me: Don't be afraid to excel," Wilson said about his sister. "And she's not at all. She's reaching for the stars, and she'll touch them and keep going."

"Russell is my best friend but also my role model," Anna told ESPN.

"I want to be a Christian man who helps lead and helps change lives and helps serve other people," Wilson said. "It's not about me, and it's about just helping other people."

The desire to serve comes from the faith he embraced as a teen and remains dedicated to today.

"My faith is everything," Wilson said. "God comes first, family and friends come second, and football comes third. I think when you keep it in that order, great things happen to you."

"I am only one, but still, I am one. I cannot do everything, but I can do something. And, because I cannot do everything, I will not refuse to do what I can."

—EDWARD EVERETT HALE

obligation   boundness
trust   restraint

RESPONSIBILITY

answerability

importance

culpability   power

subjection   contract

engagement   duty

> *"The price of greatness is responsibility."*
>
> **WINSTON CHURCHILL**

STEPH CURRY

»FACTOIDS

His real name is Wardell Stephen Curry II, named after his father.

His mother fines him $100 for every turnover above three each game.

Every so often a truly great player comes into a sport. These are the athletes who become legends for their talent and performance. Think of LeBron James, Michael Phelps, and Tom Brady. Throughout history they become part of the pantheon of sports.

Rarer still is the athlete who changes the way his or her sport is played. Think Pete Maravich, Kareem Abdul-Jabbar, or Martina Navratilova.

Steph Curry may just fit in both camps.

He is perhaps the greatest shooter the NBA has ever seen. As a two-time MVP, he continues to shatter records and win titles.

Yet more than that, Curry has single-handedly changed the way basketball is played.

The man who is currently the most electrifying basketball player on earth is the same kid who was once thought to be too scrawny to do the things he has done on the court, all of which is previously unknown at the highest levels of the game.

The numbers are mind-boggling.

Over the six seasons spanning 2012 and 2017 Curry averaged 22.9, 24.0, 23.8, 30.1, 25.3, and 26.7 points. He has broken his own NBA record for most three pointers in a season twice. He hit 272 shots from long range in 2012–13, then hit 286 in 2014–15, and then topped that by draining 402 in 2015–16.

His three-point shooting percentage for his career is 43.6 percent, second in NBA history, only behind his coach, Steve Kerr. Kerr averaged one three-pointer per game during his career. Curry averages three.

He shoots nearly 48 percent from the floor and more than 90 percent from the free-throw line. He averages nearly seven assists and two steals per game. His greatness led to his winning back-to-back NBA MVP Awards in 2014–15 and 2015–16.

Like Magic, Michael, and Kobe before him, Curry has made it to single-name status. "Steph" is known around the world. Fans congregate an hour before games when Steph comes to town so they can witness the shooting display, similar to the fans in the Bronx who watch Aaron Judge take batting practice. Curry is a bona fide basketball rock star.

"I dreamed about being an NBA player and being successful," Curry said, "but I never thought I'd get this far or understand the situation going on right now. It's been a whirlwind."

Within the last decade, complaints were commonplace among coaches, general managers, scouts, and even media and fans on the poor shooting of most NBA players. The talk was about how outside shooting was a thing of the past. And then came Steph.

Like Pete Maravich, a revolutionary star before him, Curry's range is seemingly unlimited—sometimes from 30 or even 40 feet—and he is a threat to score whenever he has the ball in his hands.

Writers used to say of Maravich that he was open as soon as he got off the bus.

"Off the dribble, without a pass, he's the best I've ever seen," said Steph's dad, Dell Curry, himself a former NBA star.[1]

Dell, now a television analyst for the Charlotte Hornets, was one of the great shooters of his generation. He used to play one-on-one with Steph on a regular basis, that is, until Steph beat him when he was a high school senior. They haven't played since.

And while his dad is right about Curry's adeptness at shooting off the dribble, it's not just off the dribble that he is lethal. It's pull-up jumpers in the lane. Coming off a pick, fighting through double teams, spot-up jumpers—it's all the same. He can make any shot from anywhere on the court at any time.

"The Lord has blessed me with these talents to do something special," Curry said. "But it's not about me. Winning games, losing games, missing shots, making shots, it doesn't matter. It's all about giving glory to God.

"I want people to know when they see me play that something is different, that I play for something different, and whether I'm talking about it [or not], I just hope by the way I carry myself and by the way I play the game, they can see there's something different about that guy."

Curry has always seemed comfortable with who he is. He has been able to easily and authentically communicate his faith.

"It's very humbling to know I'm able to be on the stage that I am," he told *Sports Spectrum*. "I think God has put me in this situation to change this perspective on what it is to be a man of God and a player in the NBA. I want to use the gifts God gave me on the basketball court to uplift His name. That's at the forefront of why I play the game.

"When I pound my chest and point to the sky, it symbolizes that I have a heart for God, something my mom and I came up with in college. I do it every time I step on the court as a reminder of who I'm playing for. People should know who I represent and why I am who I am, and that's because of my Lord and Savior."[2]

In 2015 he released the Curry One shoe by Under Armour, which had "I can do all things" inscribed on the inside tongue of the sneaker, quoting Philippians 4:13 (NKJV): "I can do all things through Christ who strengthens me."

"You don't want to scare people away with this idea that I'm perfect or that you have to be perfect to find that calling," Curry told a group of reporters in 2015. "It means a lot to be able to spread that message, whether that's what you believe or whether it helps you find whatever it is that motivates you to do all things. Every time you put on the shoe, it's a good reminder of what is possible."

Curry is a firm believer that all things are possible. All he has to do is look back at the road he has traveled to get to this place.

Steph was 14 years old when Dell retired in 2002. His father gave him a love for basketball.

"I loved being around my dad. Every kid wants to do what his parents do. I always had a ball in my hand," says Curry, who wears his dad's jersey number (30).

Curry used to accompany his dad to practice and play shooting games with Dell's teammates.

"All my teammates realized he could shoot the ball at a very young age," Dell said.[3]

Twice all-state in high school, Curry attracted no interest from any of the major basketball programs. They were scared off by his size. He was just six feet and 160 pounds at the time. He landed at Davidson College, a small Division I school.

Three years later he was a two-time All-American, the NCAA's single-season three-point record holder, and the school's all-time leading scorer. He led Davidson to their greatest sports moment when they upset three teams to make it to the Elite Eight of the NCAA Men's Tournament.

Even then his NBA future was uncertain. Predraft assessments included critiques such as "extremely small for an NBA shooting guard" and "not a natural point guard an NBA team can rely on."

Ignoring those concerns, the Golden State Warriors drafted him seventh in the first round, hoping he would fill out. He eventually did, and after three seasons of fighting through an ankle injury, Curry exploded during the 2012–13 season.

The player they call the "Baby-Faced Assassin" was then on his way to stardom. The kid who nobody wanted was suddenly managing endless autograph lines, soaring jersey and sneaker sales, a need for personal bodyguards, and a few rounds of golf with President Obama.

While success seemed to come suddenly for Curry, that depreciates the work he put in to become great and continues to put in to become greater.

"I think you have the gene to shoot, but you also have to have the gene to work at it," Dell said. "You can have skill, but if you don't work at it, it's not going to get better."[4]

"I've always been a believer that the Lord has put whatever talent in you, [and] whatever gift He has put in you, He wants you to get the most out of that. He wants you to succeed. He wants you to pursue and work and be passionate about it," Curry said. "It's not about getting any of the glory for yourself. It's all for His [glory]. That's where you have to keep perspective. Work at it and do all you can so you get the most out of yourself, but do it for His will."

Case in point, after the 2014–15 season, when he led the Warriors to the NBA title, Curry became the first Warriors player in 55 years to win the MVP Award. The next season he won the award again. But as Paul Harvey used to say, here's the rest of the story.

In his repeat MVP performance, Curry was even better than the previous season. He led the league in scoring at 30.1 points per game to go along with 6.7 assists and 5.4 rebounds. He put on what may be the greatest shooting exhibition in basketball history over a full season, hitting more than 50 percent of his shots from the floor, 45.4 percent from beyond the three-point arc, and 90.8 percent at the free-throw line. It made total sense that he would be the MVP. Yet in winning his second trophy Curry did something no one else had ever done in the history of the league: He was a unanimous selection for MVP. Think about it. Bill Russell, Wilt Chamberlain, Kareem Abdul-Jabbar, Larry Bird, Magic Johnson, Michael Jordan, Kobe Bryant, LeBron James. Not one of them—not one—had ever been the unanimous MVP. That is, until Steph in 2015–16. But that's not all.

Curry finished fourth in the voting for the league's most improved player. Think about that for a moment. The reigning league MVP almost won the MIP. He was the only player ever to average 30 points while playing fewer than 35 minutes per game. *And he got better!* Which is why he was the unanimous choice for MVP.

Those who know Curry best are amazed at how little all of this has changed him. He still says "yes, sir" and "no, sir." He signs every autograph. And he uses his platform to reach out to those in need.

Dell says that when he's working a Hornets game, people will come up to him and comment on Steph's character.

"Refs and officials come up to me all the time," said Dell, "and they say, 'Not only is your boy a great player, he's a great person.' I'm very proud of him.[5]

"Basketball will stop one day, but the person you are, you'll be for the rest of your life. He's a great person, very respectful."[6]

"The Spirit of God and the love of God just exude through that boy," Steph's mom, Sonya, told *Sports Spectrum*. "He makes everybody he meets feel special. He doesn't overlook anyone."[7]

For Steph, it all seems natural, even organic to who he is. Yet he still feels a sense of responsibility.

"He [God] has given me a lot of responsibility," he said. "I'm in a different demographic than most of the players and most of my teammates. Totally different situation. Different priorities. Different interests. Me, personally, battling being a part of the team and not being the odd ball out—that's the hardest thing to balance. My priority is to be a man and child of God and not get sucked into the temptations a lot of guys don't have a problem getting into. Family definitely helps me in that regard, because if my faith carries them and they're happy, I know I'm doing the right thing."

For Curry, part of doing the right things means helping others, a responsibility he is passionate about. He and his wife, Ayesha, were married in 2011 and started a family the following year. They also launched a number of charitable works.

Among them is a partnership with an organization called Nothing But Nets, founded by writer Rick Reilly. It is part of the United Nations Foundation's effort to combat malaria around the world. The nonprofit distributes nets in Africa to protect people from malaria, which causes more than 600,000 deaths a year in Africa, according to the World Health Organization.

Through his own Three-for-Three Challenge, Curry donates three nets (which cost ten dollars for three) for every three-pointer he made during an individual season. With more than 1,500 three-pointers over the past five years, that's a lot of nets. In 2013 he traveled with Reilly to Africa to hang the nets too. He spent his summer vacation in some mud huts in Tanzania, visiting with the people and bringing hope.

"I picked nets because it's a way people can make a huge difference right away," he told Reilly. "We can really save kids' lives. I've seen it now. I'll never forget it."[8]

It is all part of Curry being who he feels he was created to be: a game changer.

"He is doing an incredible job," Ayesha said. "I can't begin to tell you everything—how I wake up and see how amazing and strong he is. He really is changing the stereotype of an NBA player. A lot of that has to do with the way he was raised. It also has to do with a lot of the decisions he made in his life. There is just really no option. It's the way we live. It's who we are, and it's what we represent."[9]

> *"Our duty is to be useful, not according to
> our desires, but according to our powers."*
>
> **HENRI-FRÉDÉRIC AMIEL**

MAYA DIRADO

She was a classic underdog. A first-time Olympian who did not have quite the international résumé of the other women in the pool. Yet Madeline "Maya" DiRado had something her competitors overlooked: quiet confidence. She also had unmeasurable heart and determination, an iron will. And she peaked at just the right time.

Heading into the 2016 Rio Olympics, Maya's name was lost amid those of Michael Phelps, Katie Ledecky, and Missy Franklin. But her story turned out to be one of the most thrilling and successful of the games.

After narrowly missing qualifying for the 2012 games, DiRado spent four years training and pushing herself toward 2016 even as she was finishing her studies at Stanford and preparing for a career. It paid off. At the 2016 U.S. Olympic Trials, she exploded, winning three individual events. While she may have been a bit under the radar on the international scene, there were plenty of people familiar with the U.S. swim team who expected Maya to surprise in Rio.

The Santa Rosa, California, native lived up to those expectations. She was part of the 4x200-meter freestyle relay team that won gold. She won a silver 400-meter individual medley and a bronze in the 200-meter individual medley. She saved her best for last, though, capping off her amazing performance with a come-from-behind, gut-it-out performance to capture gold in her final event: the 200-meter backstroke.

Hungary's Katinka Hosszú was favored to win the event and led the entire race until DiRado surged and caught her with less than 25 meters to go, out-touching Hosszú at the wall by six one-hundredths of a second in one of the most thrilling races of the games.

"The emotions definitely came out as soon as I finished," DiRado said.

To finish her career with a gold medal, she continued, was "the perfect way to go out."

Go out, as in finished, done. DiRado had decided before the games that her swimming career would be over after the Olympics, no matter the results. She had already accepted a job with McKinsey and Company, an elite global management firm in Atlanta. She and her husband planned to move and start their lives there as soon as the games ended.

In the afterglow of her gold medal victory, DiRado was a picture of pure joy while exhibiting extraordinary humility and graciousness toward her competitors.

Then, again, this is no ordinary young woman.

DiRado (who got the name Maya from her sister, who could not pronounce Madeline) skipped second grade, started high school at age 13, made a perfect score on the math SAT at age 15, and entered Stanford at age 17.

She started swimming at age six and became a three-time high school state champion in the 200-meter intermediate medley. As a high school senior, she set the California state record in the event.

After graduating with a degree in management science and engineering, she secured a consulting job prior to the Olympics that began shortly after the games ended.

Impressive, yes. As was her perspective in victory.

"I don't think God really cares about my swimming very much," Maya told Yahoo Sports. "This is not my end purpose, to make the Olympic team. My God is powerful and in control, but I don't think He cares whether I win. It's interesting theology you can get into when it's a God of victory in your sport.

"I think God cares about my soul and whether I'm bringing His love and mercy into the world. Can I be a loving, supportive teammate, and can I bless others around me in the same way God has been so generous with me?"[1]

Medals were never Maya's motivation. Rather, she was driven by the constant desire to be better and to see what she could draw out of herself.

"As I got to know Maya better, one thing that surprised me was what motivates her," Greg Meehan, her coach at Stanford, told the *Washington Post*. "It was never about being competitive or trying to win. It was always about being the best she could be, to find her own version of perfection. She's also the smartest person I've ever coached."[2]

"I'm motivated by seeing how good I can be," Maya told *Christianity Today* during the 2016 games. "That applies not just at race time but during every practice. Am I preparing as well as I possibly can? I set high goals for myself and then enjoy the process of working toward them."[3]

This perspective was reinforced by her parents and her husband, also a competitive swimmer.

"Their biggest role was reminding me that success is whether I prepared and executed as well as I possibly could," DiRado said. "It's never been about winning or beating other people." Knowing she had a husband, a job, and a new life waiting after the games allowed DiRado to swim freely, without pressure. This made the competition at the Rio games fun for her because the end was in sight.

"It's so much easier to work hard every day and push myself and be excited about all the little things that make swimming great but are kind of hard to get excited about when you're looking at this like, 'Oh, I have so many more years ahead of me doing this,'" DiRado told the *Washington Post*.[4]

"It may be hard for some people to understand, but I'd rather go out on a high with this amazing experience than to continue until I hate it or I'm no longer competing at a high level," she said. "I'll have absolutely no regrets about what could have been."

That understanding has helped DiRado to take her focus off herself in a sport that is mostly centered on the individual.

"My faith has helped me remember that there are so many more important things in life worth doing. Swimming is a pretty selfish activity, and so I've always known that it can't be my whole world."

Today, age 23 is young for an elite swimmer, even a prime career age.

DiRado could have turned her Olympic success into a career for a few more years. She was getting faster in the pool, had secured a sponsorship, and was at the peak of her success.

Yet a long career in swimming is not for everyone. The training is grueling and includes early mornings and late nights. Even though DiRado was performing at the highest level of her career and seemed to be getting faster, her decision to leave swimming seemed even more on target. The reason: She became bored with swimming.

While Maya was clearly emotional after her victories in Rio, she maintained a healthy perspective on what she had achieved as she closed out a very successful chapter of her life. She was ready for what came next.

"Knowing that I'm a child of God and that His love for me is determined by nothing I can achieve or do on my own has given me a quiet confidence," she said. "I think my faith has helped me chart my own course and pursue my goals when people around me may be going in different directions."

Before she left, however, DiRado made a point of consoling Missy Franklin, the reigning Olympic champion and world record holder, who failed to qualify for the final in Rio. At the end of their heat, DiRado scanned the scoreboard and saw Franklin's time, knowing it was not enough to make the final. She swam over to the teary Franklin and comforted her, telling her what a great teammate she had been and that she was loved by the entire team.

The gesture was a powerful display of compassion to Franklin.

"For her to support me in the way she has is so incredible," Franklin said.

Everyone else knew it was just Maya being Maya.

*"We cannot do everything at once,
but we can do something at once."*

CALVIN COOLIDGE

JRUE AND LAUREN HOLIDAY

It has been said that the greatest expression of love is sacrifice.

Sacrifice and love were at the heart of New Orleans Pelicans guard Jrue Holiday's decision when his wife was faced with a devastating health challenge. His wife, in turn, made a sacrifice of her own.

In 2016 Lauren Holiday, a two-time Olympic gold medalist for the U.S. women's national soccer team, was diagnosed with a benign tumor on the right side of her brain. Holiday had recently retired from soccer to start a family and was six months pregnant. Consistent, painful headaches led doctors to find the tumor.

"Devastating," said Jrue, of the diagnosis.

The couple and their doctors consulted to determine the best course of action. Brain surgery was necessary, and the sooner the better.

Lauren had a meningioma, the most common type of tumor that forms in the head, according to the Mayo Clinic. Most meningiomas are benign but can be severely disabling if they continue to grow and are left untreated, according to the American Association of Neurological Surgeons. Lauren was already experiencing numbness on the right side of her head and face.

In an uncommon move, Jrue and Lauren chose to wait until their unborn daughter reached eight months to induce labor and then have the surgery. Lauren, who underwent open-heart surgery to fix a congenital defect at the age of three, made the courageous decision. She was determined to give birth to a healthy baby, even if it imperiled her own health.

"She's obviously a fighter, the toughest woman I know," Jrue said. "That's the reason why I married her."

Then came Jrue's sacrifice. The timing of the procedure pushed it and Lauren's recovery well into the NBA regular season. The NBA All-Star and defensive standout made the decision to leave the team for an indefinite period to care for his wife and newborn, thereby postponing his start to the 2016–17 season.

"My family comes before basketball," he said. "I'm obviously blessed to play this game and be in the position I am in, but my wife is the most important thing in the world to me. She comes before anything else."

Jrue and Lauren met when at UCLA. Jrue starred on the Bruins basketball team, and Lauren did the same on the women's soccer team. Jrue was drafted by the Philadelphia 76ers, and Lauren was selected for the U.S. national team. They married in 2013, and in July of that year Jrue was traded from the 76ers to the Pelicans.

Lauren was part of the U.S. team that won gold medals at the 2008 Olympics in Beijing and in 2012 at the London games and also won the FIFA Women's World Cup title in 2015. She was named the National Women's Soccer League's MVP in 2013, and the U.S. Soccer Federation honored her in 2014 as its Female Athlete of the Year.

In 2015, at the height of her career, Lauren retired from soccer so she and Jrue could start a family.

Her pregnancy went smoothly until the headaches started. An MRI revealed the tumor on the right side of her brain, near her orbital socket. Second opinions confirmed the diagnosis.

"Obviously, we were still very excited about the birth of our first child, but our focus shifted from having this magnificent blessing to making sure everything is going to be okay with Lauren and the child," Jrue said.

Jrue met with Pelicans general manager Dell Demps and head coach Alvin Gentry to outline a plan. The team was supportive of their star player's decision, even though they had no idea how long he might be away.

"We told Jrue to forget about the basketball part of it," said Gentry. "This is where you take care of your family."[1]

"There wasn't any pressure to be with the team or to choose between my team and my wife," Jrue said. "They told me to be a husband first. I don't think they know how much their support means to me and my family."

Jrue remained on the Pelicans active roster throughout his time off so he would be able to come back whenever the time was right.

Lauren was induced a month early and gave birth to a healthy daughter—Jrue Tyler—at Duke University Hospital in September 2016.

About six weeks later Lauren was back at the Duke hospital to undergo surgery to remove the tumor. The Holidays relied on their faith for strength.

"There's nothing in life my wife can't conquer with Jesus Christ in her corner," Jrue tweeted prior to the surgery.

"I fully believe they can handle this situation because of how good they are and how great their faith is," Pelicans forward Quincy Pondexter told the *New Orleans Times-Picayune* at the time.[2]

"They are two great people, two great athletes, and understanding what they were going through, it was really tough," said Gentry. "I will say this. If you had to choose a person to go through this, it would be Lauren Holiday. She's a very, very tough individual."

The procedure was performed in November 2016. Doctors told the Holidays the surgery was successful and they felt that Lauren would return to a completely normal life.

After the surgery the Holidays took up residence in the Raleigh-Durham area for the foreseeable future to be near Lauren's medical team. Both Jrue's and Lauren's families spent extended time with the family to help. The Pelicans had an athletic trainer work with Jrue for the months the family was in North Carolina to maintain his skills and conditioning.

By December 2016 Lauren was doing well enough that Jrue announced he was going to rejoin the Pelicans. He spent three months as Lauren's primary caretaker and waited until she was at a point where she could take care of herself and the baby. He returned to basketball with his wife's blessing.

Lauren's road to recovery was difficult. Early in 2017 she shared about her difficult journey on Instagram. "I have never quite known suffering like I experienced the last six months," she wrote. "I can remember count-less nights repeating, 'There may be pain in the night, but joy comes in the morning.' I remember half believing it and half still in disbelief that this was my life. I memorized Scripture, and some days my faith felt unshak-able and others I was scared to death."

She went on to say that along with her faith and her family, what helped her get through was her newborn daughter. "Every time I see this smile, I'm reminded that joy does come in the morning."

Then, in May 2017, in honor of Mother's Day, Lauren posted another comment, also sharing a photo of herself wearing a "Girl Power" T-shirt. Her post read: "I have been hiding myself from a camera for the past seven months. I didn't want anyone to see my paralyzed face, my eye that is now crossed, the bald spots from radiation and my half-shaved head. Granted, you can't see any of those things in this picture, just a patch… it's a huge step. Today reminded me just how incredibly strong women are. The resilience of our bodies, the power of our minds, the ability to put other humans fully before ourselves, our compassionate hearts, but most of all our undying love for our families, our friends, and our pre-cious babies. I am so proud to be a daughter, a sister, an aunt, a wife, and, most of all, a mother."

Lauren has navigated her recovery and a return to a healthy life. Jrue has shined in his return to the court, playing his best basketball in the 2017–18 season. Yet as he has demonstrated, his success on the court is insignificant in comparison to having a healthy wife and child.

"You can get through anything with God," Jrue said. "My wife is doing really well, and that's all I can ask for. She's alive, and I'm blessed for that. My daughter is okay. So I'm happy."

"The questions for each man to settle is not what he would do if he had the means, time, influence, and educational advantages, but what he will do with the things he has."

HAMILTON WRIGHT MABIE

DANIEL MURPHY

» FACTOIDS

His boyhood hero was San Diego Padres Hall of Famer Tony Gwynn.

His wife, Tori, was a star softball pitcher at the University of North Florida.

Daniel Murphy is known as a professional hitter. At every level of this baseball experience, he has hit the ball well.

As a throwback to an earlier era of baseball, the Washington Nationals second baseman brings a dedication to his craft that recalls the likes of Ted Williams, Wade Boggs, George Brett, and Rod Carew. While others may have had more of the art of hitting down, Murphy excels in the science of a bat hitting a ball. Few hitters in the game today carry more focus into the batter's box with each at-bat.

"I try to see what the pitcher is featuring and where he's going to look to try to get me out, and then leverage that with where I'd like to get a pitch to hit and formulate a game plan," Murphy said.

"I really like hitting the ball on the barrel [of the bat]," Murphy told *Sports Illustrated*. "It's fun. When you center a ball, it's just a really clean feeling."[1]

Few hitters have experienced that feeling as often as Murphy. Heading into the 2018 season, he had become a three-time All-Star and had won two Silver Slugger awards. With a career batting average of .299, Murphy has gotten better with age.

As a member of the New York Mets from 2008 to 2015, his record-breaking performance in the 2015 postseason thrust him into the national spotlight. It also provided the impetus for his making some changes to his hitting approach that would lift him to another level the following two seasons.

It started in the fall of 2015, when the Mets made the playoffs. What ensued was a historic run of at-bats for Murphy in leading his team into the World Series.

Murphy put his name in the Major League Baseball record books as the first player ever to hit a home run in six consecutive postseason games, doing so against the Los Angeles Dodgers in the NL Divisional Series and the Chicago Cubs in the NL Championship Series. The feat was made more impressive by the list of pitchers he took deep during the streak: Clayton Kershaw (twice), Zack Greinke, Jake Arrieta, Jon Lester, Kyle Hendricks, and Fernando Rodney—six pitchers with a combined five Cy Young awards. He batted a ridiculous .556 against Chicago and was named series MVP. Over the two playoff series, Murphy clubbed seven homers and drove in 11 runs.

"My wife didn't grow up with baseball like we did," Murphy's brother Jonathan said in recalling his brother's homer barrage. "So when he kept hitting them, she was just like, 'Is this normal? What's going on?' I said, 'No, this is not normal! This never happens!' It was pretty wild for everyone, Daniel included. I don't think he really knew what was going on either."[2]

"The more notoriety I got, I tried to push in closer to Jesus," Murphy, a Christian, told *Sports Spectrum*. "I didn't want to take that glory for myself. It was a really, really sweet time in our lives."[3]

What followed was not quite as sweet. During the World Series, Murphy struggled. He hit just .150 and did not drive in a run. He struck out seven times and made two costly errors in the field.

"Being on top of the mountain and then being at the bottom of the barrel…just felt like a perfect picture of God's grace and love in our lives," Murphy said. "Jesus didn't love me any less when I made those errors in the World Series than He did when I was hitting those home runs in the NLCS.

"If anything, He loved me more in the midst of [the World Series], because if He didn't think our family could handle that kind of struggle, He wouldn't have allowed it to happen in our lives. I felt Him saying, 'I think you can handle this, and on My strength, you're going to grow from this, and you're going to be stronger, and I'm going to refine your heart and the heart of your family in the midst of struggle.'"

The World Series performance did little to change Murphy's reputation. When the season ended, his contract was up. The Mets offered him $18 million for a one-year contract. Murphy wanted a longer-term deal. When the Nationals gave him a three-year offer for $37.5 million, Murphy took it, passing up more money per year for the stability.

He rewarded the Nationals well, terrorizing National League pitchers in 2016, hitting .347 with 25 home runs and 104 RBI. He led the league in doubles with 47 as well as in slugging percentage and OPS, and he struck out in less than 9 percent of his plate appearances. The career-high numbers put Murphy second in the NL MVP vote.

He continued the assault in 2017, slamming 23 homers, driving in 93 runs, and hitting .322 while again leading the league with 43 doubles and again receiving MVP consideration. At the age of 32, he had arrived as one of the most feared and productive hitters in the game.

Then, again, Murphy has always been most comfortable with a bat in his hands.

Murphy was practically raised to hit a baseball. As a child in Jacksonville, Florida, he and his two siblings spent years at Smitty's Learning Center. The local day care facility was run by a couple who had sons of their own, and the husband had a small baseball field with a batting cage.

"As long as you would throw the baseball to him," Murphy's father, Tom, told *FCA* magazine, "he would swing the bat all day long."[4]

He ended up going to Jacksonville University, where he was far advanced as a hitter.

"He was ahead of the game," his former Jacksonville coach Terry Alexander told *FCA* magazine. "It was more of a professional approach."[5]

As a junior in 2006, Murphy hit .398 and was named the Atlantic Sun Conference player of the year. The Mets made him their thirteenth-round draft choice. He reached the big leagues for the final third of the season in 2008, hitting .313.

The biggest problem for Murphy was trying to find a position for him.

With all the work he did in the batting cage, he had not mastered a position in the field, rotating mostly between outfield and third base. When he made it to the majors, Murphy was shuttled between left field, third base, first base, and second base, eventually settling there. But not without detractors who were critical of his defensive ability.

Life as an athlete, especially in New York, has one constant: critics. One's play is analyzed and overanalyzed by beat writers, television reporters, bloggers, and radio talk show hosts. There is no shortage of criticism.

Criticism was consistent in New York regarding Murphy's lack of power, which changed in 2015. He was labeled a defensive liability. In 2014 the critics had been especially harsh when Murphy announced he would miss the season opener to be with his wife, Tori, when she gave birth to their first child.

"She wanted me to be there, and I wanted to be there," he said. "That was a decision that we made as a family."

Radio personalities blistered him, saying he belonged on the field, not with his wife. But Murphy's decision had the support of his teammates and manager Terry Collins. Fans had his back too, as did President Barack Obama, who invited Murphy to speak at a Working Families Summit at the White House.

After his son, Noah, was born, Murphy went back to doing what he does best: hitting.

"Hitting to me is trying to set attainable goals," Murphy said. "What's an attainable goal? A base hit is not an attainable goal. It's outside of your control. But being prepared, being ready to hit, and getting a good pitch in your zone and getting your A-swing off, that's attainable. So hopefully, I try to do that 550 to 600 times a year."

In 2015 Mets hitting coach Kevin Long convinced Murphy to tweak the swing he had spent more than a quarter century perfecting. After all, with his unceasing work ethic, phenomenal hand-eye coordination, and pinpoint precision, Murphy already was a hitting machine.

"His eyes and hands work as well as any human being on the planet," Mets scout Steve Barningham (the one who discovered Murphy), told *Sports Illustrated*. "If he sees it, he can hit it."[6]

Still, Long believed if Murphy sat lower in his stance, his balance would improve, and an adjustment in his hand positioning and foot plant would improve his timing. He told Murphy the changes would transform him from a high average hitter to a true slugger. Murphy listened and it worked.

To his credit, while he admits to being adamantly stubborn, Murphy is teachable. That, he says, comes from his faith.

"If I were to write out the perfect plan, it never would have worked out like this—ever," Murphy told *FCA* magazine. "God put things in my life with my family that just tried to strip away the massive idol that is baseball as I mold, hopefully, into a gracious and serving husband and father.

"Just like any other profession, it's easy for us to want to measure our self-worth, value and identity by our work. I'm keenly aware of the fact that I want to derive value from my statistics, but that's not where my self-worth is, that's not where my value is. My goal isn't base hits; it's holiness. I know that any good thing you see coming out of me is Jesus."[7]

When the team is at home, Murphy and his wife lead a Bible study for his teammates and their wives. The commitment comes out of a lesson he learned from Mets chaplain Cali Magallenes.

"He told me, 'There will be two people waiting for you when you get done with the game of baseball,'" Murphy told *FCA* magazine. "'One of them I know will be there, and that'll be Jesus. And the other one will be your wife. The relationship you have with her will be a direct result of the investment you've made in her over the course of these years.'"[8]

On road trips, Murphy's room is the place where the players get together to encourage one another and study the Bible.

"There's so much isolation in baseball," he said. "There's so much isolation everywhere...So in an effort to get together and sharpen each other, [several of us] try to meet once a road trip. It's an opportunity get into the [Bible] and study and talk about what's going on.

"I want to build relationships and hopefully show people I'm far from perfect, but I know where there's hope and where there's joy and where there's peace...and I want to point them in that direction."

CARSON WENTZ

» FACTOIDS

His favorite football player growing up was Brett Favre.

His favorite food is steak.

When Carson Wentz was selected as the second overall pick in the 2016 NFL draft, it marked the culmination of a remarkable journey for the man the Philadelphia Eagles were hoping would be their franchise quarterback.

North Dakota State is not exactly the place NFL teams have been known to go to find the man who will be the face of their franchise. Then again, this is no ordinary man.

Wentz is a unique athlete, possessing all the physical attributes to be a star player in the league. More than that, he demonstrates a maturity that far exceeds his age. It's clear Wentz is comfortable in his own skin. Something that may not have been so true ten years ago.

When Wentz reported for the first day of football practice as a freshman at Century High School in Bismarck, North Dakota, he stood five-feet-eight and was 125 pounds soaking wet, as they say. Though he always knew he was meant to be a quarterback, he played receiver and linebacker until his junior year. After injuries took most of his junior year, by the time he was a senior, Wentz had grown to six-feet-five and 200 pounds, and he won the job as the varsity quarterback.

"I came out of nowhere my senior year," Wentz told *Sports Spectrum*.

"That's why I was passed over by some of the larger schools and ended up at North Dakota State."[1]

At NDSU Wentz developed into an NFL quarterback. It was also there that he was encouraged, by a teammate, to go deeper in his faith. That teammate, Dante Perez, worked to surround Wentz with other players who were men of faith and solid character. Two years later Wentz was the starting quarterback. After Perez graduated, Wentz knew it was his turn to go from mentee to mentor.

"After having these guys pour into me, I started pouring into younger guys as well," Wentz told *Sports Spectrum*. "I had earned the respect of others through my position on the team, and I felt called to really open up to guys and let them open up to me. I wanted them to know that I cared for them—that I was more than just their quarterback. Discipling others is one of the most rewarding things I've ever done. Sitting in the dining hall having conversations about faith with Christians and non-Christians alike was amazing."[2]

On the field, he was developing as well.

"I knew I could play, and so did my teammates," Wentz said. "I'd been blessed with the talent, but I hadn't yet had the chance to really play. When I finally got that chance, I ran with it."

In his first year as a starter in 2014, as a junior, Wentz led NDSU to the national championship. NFL scouts began to take notice of the six-foot-five redhead with a rocket arm, supreme athleticism, and cool leadership.

During his senior season, scouts populated the sidelines and the press box. Agents called. Wentz tried to block it all out and keep his focus on the field. Then, in the sixth game of the season, disaster struck.

"I'd broken my throwing wrist," Wentz told *Sports Spectrum*. "I didn't know if I would be able to throw again. And even if I could, I wondered, 'Did I do enough this season to get drafted?' I felt sorry for myself for about five minutes and then I let go of the anger and frustration and just started praying. By no means was this easy—there was a chance that my football career was over—but I knew that God had a plan for even this. I need to lean into God and trust *His* plan."[3]

While his team continued winning, Wentz healed. When NDSU made it back to the national championship game, he was faced with a decision. It was really a no-brainer for Wentz. With his wrist not completely healed, Wentz chose to quarterback the Bison in the championship game, risking further injury and his NFL career. NDSU won 37–10, and Wentz was named the game's MVP.

"There's no way I was going to let that opportunity pass me by," he said. "That could have been the last game of my career—and it would have been a storybook ending."

Alas, sports do not always offer storybook endings. Such was the case in the 2017 season.

After starting all 16 games as a rookie in 2016, throwing for 3,782 yards and 16 touchdowns, Wentz gave the Eagles a leg up on the rest of the NFC in 2017 as they were picked as favorites to go to the Super Bowl. They were on their way until that leg up came down.

During a December game against the Los Angeles Rams, Wentz suffered a torn ACL when he was hit as he scrambled into the end zone. He had to have surgery and was lost for the rest of what was a magical season.

The Eagles were 13-2, had clinched the NFC East, and were the prohibitive favorite to head to the Super Bowl. Wentz was being touted as the favorite for NFL MVP, having thrown for nearly 3,300 yards and 33 touchdowns in 13 games.

Through the disappointment, Wentz went to his Twitter page after the game to thank the fans for the prayers and well wishes that had been sent to him via social media. He posted: "I greatly appreciate all the prayers! I know my God is a powerful one with a perfect plan. Time to just lean in to Him and trust whatever the circumstances!"

He then shared Proverbs 3:5-6: "Trust in the Lord with all your heart and lean not on your own understanding. In all your ways acknowledge Him and He will make your path straight."

Wentz then became the Eagles most fervent cheerleader as they won Super Bowl LII.

This is the Carson Wentz everyone had known since college. He remains driven by the thought that he plays simply for an audience of one. The phrase "audience of one" became a maxim of sorts for Wentz. He had AO1 tattooed on his right wrist to serve as a reminder of what his career and his life are all about.

"It was kind of a motto I picked up early in my career, and I finally put it on my body just to live with the Lord as my audience," Wentz said.

The phrase became so central to Wentz that he has begun to use it as a sort of brand that tells who he is. He wore cleats during the season with the AO1 logo on it, and he has the logo stamped on all of his social media and on the attire he wears to press conferences.

At its heart, the slogan reflects Wentz's humility and his call to others to play only for God. As part of his desire to live out this mission, Wentz launched an Audience of One Foundation.

The foundation exists "to demonstrate the love of God by providing opportunities and support for the less fortunate and those in need."

The AO1 Foundation has supported Mission of Hope to help launch a sports initiative in Haiti to develop youth, reinforce education, and invest in the next generation of leaders. Haitian children will have access to tutoring, food, shelter, and electrical power. Wentz became passionate about helping when he took a trip to Haiti after the 2016 season.

"You can see pictures. You can see videos of this place, but [it's not] until you're there that it really hits you," Wentz told the Eagles website. "That's exactly what it did for me being there, seeing the gravel roads and all these kids. Barely any of them have shoes. They're just running around. They didn't care. They're kicking plastic bottles because they don't have a soccer ball. Their clothes didn't fit; kids' pants are falling down. They're trying to hold them up, but they're still playing soccer, laughing, having a blast. It's just a different environment for sure. I don't think anyone should be living this way, but happiness was there too."[4]

So there you have it. The face of the Eagles franchise, the star quarterback in a major media market, the hope for Philly fans is really just a guy who loves to hunt almost as much as he loves football and thinks about others rather than himself. As he prepares for the 2018 season and beyond, he is staying focused on an audience of one.

"My faith throughout college made me patient as I waited my turn," he says. "It got me through my injury without a doubt. And throughout this process, it helped me to not let this thing blow up and get caught up in it all.

"I didn't know what it would look like on the Eagles. Would I fit in? Would there be other Christians on my team? What would the locker room be like? I look back and realize that even my best expectations were blown out of the water. I couldn't ask for a better situation."

"Freedom and constraint are two aspects of the same necessity, the necessity of being the man you are and not another. You are free to be that man, but not another."

—ANTOINE DE SAINT-EXUPERY

refraining moderation
avoidance
SELF-CONTROL
forbearance
self-restraint
temperance chastity
soberness
non-indulgence
abstaining
self-denial

> *"Conquering others requires force.*
> *Conquering oneself requires strength."*

LAO TZU

DEREK CARR

> **» FACTOIDS**
>
> His middle name is Dallas because his mom was born just outside of Dallas, Texas.
>
> His favorite food is a protein shake.

When the Oakland Raiders made Derek Carr their top draft pick at the start of the second round in 2014, the Raiders leadership felt they had finally found their franchise quarterback.

The Raiders also made history of sorts. Carr's brother, David, was the number-one overall pick by the Houston Texans in 2002. With both brothers selected within the first thirty-six selections of the draft, they joined Peyton and Eli Manning as the only brother quarterback combos to be drafted in the first two rounds.

David is 12 years older than his brother, and Derek had learned a great deal from his older brother's NFL experience. When David was preparing for a game, watching film and studying, Derek sat with him for hours and asked a lot of questions. He wanted to know everything.

"He taught me how to compete," Carr said of his older brother. "He taught me all these things. He made it easy for me when I got my chance."

The brothers came out of Bakersfield, California, and were stars at Bakersfield Christian High School. Both then went on to star in college at Fresno State University.

During David's senior year at Fresno, he threw for more than 4,800 yards and 46 touchdowns, setting Bulldog records. The Texans, too, thought they had found their franchise quarterback after drafting him in 2002. But they forgot to put a decent offensive line in front of him. David was sacked 76 times. When he wasn't sacked, he was running for his life. Things were better in his second year he was sacked only 15 times, but the next year he went down 49 times, and the year after that 68 times. After five seasons in Houston, 249 sacks took their toll. David was battered physically and emotionally. Through it all, younger brother Derek watched, asked questions, and learned.

Twelve years after his brother had set all the Fresno records, Carr came in and erased them all. He threw for over 12,000 yards and 113 touchdowns in four seasons, as a senior passing for 5,083 yards and 50 touchdowns.

In Oakland, Carr was named the starter to open the season. He ended up throwing for 3,270 yards and 21 touchdowns with just 12 interceptions in a strong rookie season. He continued to improve, throwing for nearly 3,987 yards and 32 touchdowns in his second season and taking the Raiders into the playoffs in his third season before breaking his fibula at the end of the season. Through his first four seasons, he was selected to the Pro Bowl three times, establishing himself as one of the brightest young quarterbacks in the league.

"People say they want to be great, but they're not willing to put the time in," said Carr's oldest brother, Darren. "Derek wakes up, and if he hears about someone else waking up earlier than him, he'll set his clock back one minute. That's no joke. That's him. He's got a fire in him to be great."[1]

That fire is in great part due to Carr's family. David has been a stabilizing force and continues to be Derek's guide for life both on the field and off.

"David is so intelligent when it comes to our faith," Derek said. "He's given me some of the best advice that sticks with me all the time, some funny and some serious. On the field, off the field, the first thing he ever told me was, 'Don't be an idiot. On the field, don't be an idiot. Don't force stupid passes. Have a reason for what you're doing. And off the field, don't be an idiot. And that one's self-explanatory.'"

Part of David's counsel was to understand the time to play it safe and when to play the hero. Derek always fancied himself a hero. He used to wear Batman shirts under his uniform in high school and college.

"David had to tell him that he didn't have to be Batman all the time," said the boys' father, Rodger. "You can be Bruce Wayne for some plays. Every now and then you will need to put the cape on and make the ridiculous throw. Then you can be Batman."[2]

David's wisdom didn't end there. He's had long talks with Derek about handling both the praise and criticism that came with playing the most high-profile position in all of sports.

"People are going to say great things about you, [and] people are always going to say bad things about you," Derek recalled David telling him. "'Don't listen to either of them, because you can't get too high, you can't get too low. Say thank you, be polite, and accept it. Be thankful and grateful for it, but at the same time don't be too high and don't be too low, because as high as they put you, they can tear you down just as fast.' That's something he's taught me since I was very young."

That wisdom was important as Derek approached the 2017 season. He was coming off the fibula injury and signing a $125 million contract extension—the richest in NFL history— that made him the highest-paid player in football.

The guidance would also be important when Derek and his wife, Heather, faced their greatest crisis.

In 2013 Derek and Heather were seniors at Fresno State. They had just experienced the joy of giving birth to their first child, a son they named Dallas. As they sat with their baby boy in the hospital just after the birth, Dallas suddenly became ill. He had a potentially life-threatening intestinal condition and needed emergency surgery. The couple prayed. After Dallas came out of surgery, he became ill again and needed a second surgery. He spent 23 days in neonatal intensive care, and Derek's and Heather's faith was tested.

After being sent home with what they thought was a healthy child, the issues arose again. They rushed Dallas back to the hospital for another surgery. He has been well ever since.

"I always think about those times," Heather said. "You can still see the scar on Dallas's belly. And when you do, you just thank God that he's alive. It could have all been taken from us. That's why we cherish every moment we have as a family. We know that, no matter what happens, family will always be our top priority."[3]

"I always had my faith, but that was a real test of it," Derek told NBC Sports. "Everyone knew who we were in Fresno. It was my senior year, and everything was going great. Life was good, and we didn't worry about much. Then Dallas's ordeal came up, and it ripped my heart out. At that point, I thought, 'Am I still going to be the man I say that I am? Am I going to be strong and be there for my wife and child?' Saying those things is easy. Living and doing them can be extremely difficult.

"People wonder if bad times impact me, because I have a smile on my face. Of course they do. They rip my heart out, but I'm going to fight harder than anyone because I lean on my faith in tough times. That's where I find my strength. When a doctor says, 'Dallas might not make it,' all I can do is lean on my faith to keep from crumpling. That's all I know how to do. And I trust it's right because I've seen it come through time and time again."[4]

On social media, Derek describes himself in this order: follower of Jesus Christ, husband, father, Oakland Raider.

"When he comes home, he isn't an NFL quarterback," said Heather. "He's Dad. He's husband. We don't really talk about football at home unless he wants to. He doesn't let bad days bleed into his home life. We just get to be family."[5]

"Being a quarterback is what I do, but it does not define who I am," he wrote on his website, derekcarrqb.com. "At any moment, any second, my football career could be taken away, but my faith and relationship with God will never be taken from me."

Derek didn't always see things this way. In fact, it was Heather who helped him gain this perspective when they were friends.

"She wrote me a letter," he shared with The Increase. "And it said you're not the person I thought you were."[6]

"He would say one thing and act the opposite way," Heather said. "I thought he was so on fire for God, but then I saw the way he was living, and it just wasn't adding up."

"I remember at that moment I felt so selfish, I felt so arrogant," Derek said. "I was still a nice, genuine person, but...All of a sudden, all these feelings came upon me, and it was as if God was saying, 'Hey, I've got plans for you, and you're screwing it up.'"

"I sat down with Derek, and he apologized to me for the way he had treated me," Heather said.[7]

He said, "That next week I got up in front of my whole team and told the guys, 'I've been calling myself a Christian, and I haven't been living it. I'm a Christian now, and watch how I live now. That's what a Christian is all about.'"

After reconciling, Heather and David began dating and then engaged. They were married in 2012.

"I knew faith, family, and football were my foundation, but I wasn't living by it until I grew up and figured it out on my own," Derek said. "It wasn't people saying things to me. I found the path through experience. I've lived both ways, and I like the path I'm on a whole lot more.

"That's how I know He's with me, because I have a peace and a joy. I can't describe it, but I have it, and I know it's real."

"The sentiments of men are known not only by what they receive, but what they reject also."

THOMAS JEFFERSON

KIRK COUSINS

In 1985 Sally Field won the best actress Oscar for her role in *Places in the Heart*. Upon receiving the award, she thanked the academy and excitedly proclaimed, "You like me, right now, you like me!"

Like the members of the Academy of Motion Picture Arts and Sciences who vote for the Academy Awards, football fans and management can be fickle. One week you're celebrated, the next you're a bum.

Such is the roller-coaster life of Kirk Cousins. Over three years as a starter for the Washington Redskins, Cousins has thrown for more than 4,000 yards each season and tossed 81 touchdown passes.

He took the job from former number-one pick Robert Griffin III at the beginning of the 2015 season, and he led the Redskins from the brink of obscurity to the NFC East division title and a berth in the playoffs. In 2016 he threw for just under 5,000 yards and was named to the Pro Bowl.

Yet despite his performance, Cousins went into the 2016 and 2017 seasons with his contract ending. In 2016 the Redskins used the franchise tag on him to keep him in D.C. for one more year. In 2017 Cousins and the team were unable to work out a contract extension, and so the Redskins used the franchise tag to again keep him for another year.

As the 2017 season ended the Redskins had made no progress on signing Cousins to a long-term contract. It seemed the team was not sold enough on Cousins to commit to the money and years to keep him. All of this was puzzling, especially in light of the dearth of elite quarterbacks in the league and Cousins's track record. The cumulative effect of years of indecision and lack of job security for their quarterback appeared to create a dysfunctional environment that crippled the team's play on the field.

Thus, throughout both the 2016 and 2017 seasons, Cousins gave his all for a franchise that gave no signs of commitment in return. He was forever the bride waiting at the altar for the ring that might never come.

There were plenty of other teams standing in line, however, hoping they could slip a ring on Cousins's finger. While he was courted by the Denver Broncos, Cleveland Browns, Arizona Cardinals, and Jacksonville Jaguars, he eventually decided on the Minnesota Vikings, signing a three-year deal for a guaranteed $84 million.

For the guy called "Captain Kirk" by his teammates, who has thrown for more than 13,000 yards and 81 touchdowns in three seasons, the situation has made him feel somewhat alien. What he deserves is a Sally Fields moment—to know that his team likes and wants him.

Yet Cousins has handled all the uncertainty with grace, knowing that neither the Redskins nor another NFL team can ultimately determine his sense of self-worth or dictate his future.

"If God is in the plan, and if He is a part of the plan of me playing college football and someday playing in the NFL, a broken ankle or a setback here or there isn't going to get in the way of God's plan," Cousins told CBN News. "At the end of the day, much like my college decision, when you know that God has His hand in it and that He has a plan, it takes much of my worry and much of my doubts, and it takes them away because I trust that He brought me here for a reason."[1]

Cousins was raised in a Christian family. His father was a pastor. Cousins was homeschooled before going to Holland (Michigan) High School and then Michigan State, where he set a number of school passing records. The values instilled by his parents have formed the foundation of his life and provided a lens through which to view his circumstances. For example, to remind himself, he has a Bible passage posted in his locker.

"It's Matthew 6, verses 19 through 34. It talks about where your heart should be and what you should value in this world," Cousins explained to

WUSA TV. "It's a good [passage], a good reminder to leave it all in God's hands and trust the Lord, and He hasn't failed me yet."[2]

One of the verses in that passage reads: "But seek first the kingdom of God and his righteousness, and all these things will be added to you [ESV]."

Cousins says his faith provides the lens through which to also determine where he will end up playing. This is not a perspective that comes naturally for him.

"I'm the kind of guy who likes to have a plan and likes to have things laid out," he said. "We have to trust in the Lord's plan, and we have to walk with Him and honor Him and trust Him, and at times it's not easy. He doesn't lay out an obvious plan for us at all times, and we just have to walk by faith and trust that everything will be His best plan for us."

Before the start of the 2017 season, Cousins turned down a long-term deal from the Redskins that would have provided $53 million in guaranteed money.

"First of all, what rarely ever gets reported is that ultimately this decision is not about anything more important than my faith," Cousins told 106.7 The Fan back in July. "My faith is ultimately driving this decision. Do I feel like the Lord is leading me to make this decision or that decision, and where does He give me peace?

"He provides that compass in life to direct you and guide you and give you not only a moral compass, but just a compass in terms of wisdom to know what kind of decisions to make."[3]

Passing up that kind of money may seem unusual to the outsider. But Cousins is not driven by dollars or headlines.

"Football is very important to me and plays a huge role in my life," Cousins told *Sports Spectrum*. "It is a dream come true. But as important as football is and as passionate as I am about it, it is not the source of my identity.

"The anchor of my life is Jesus Christ. My identity is based upon His love for me and my personal relationship with Him. At the foundation of my life is His truth, as spelled out in the Bible. I am passionate about Jesus, the One who gave His life on a cross to pay for my sin. One of my greatest desires is to live a life in a way that honors Him."[4]

Because of this sense of identity, Cousins feels a sense of freedom in knowing that he is not living to please others or to gain a "You like me" moment.

Cousins is a thoughtful, polite man. He hangs photos of reporters in his locker so he can remember their names. He is also cerebral when it comes to his work. He asked the Redskins for an office so he could study film at any time. He installed a whiteboard there so he could diagram plays. He has folders stuffed with game notes in a filing cabinet so he can continue to learn his craft. Cousins knows what others have surmised, namely, that as good as he has been, he is not as good as he can become.

Cousins loves the process. He loves preparing for games as much as playing in them. His former coach, Mike Shanahan, told Cousins he felt he could become a Super Bowl–winning quarterback. He told the Redskins brass they should either make Cousins the starter or trade him, as it was clear to him that Cousins would beat Griffin out.

Cousins hired a brain coach in 2011. This coach found that Cousins's brain speeds up when he encounters significant danger. To help his brain get into the perfect range, Cousins trained with a program that plays movies, slowing them down to slow down his brain.

The attention to process, to training his brain, to deeper study, and to proper sleep (more on that later) have all been part of Cousins evolution into the quarterback he has become, which is the third-most accurate passer in NFL history.

"Process relaxes me," he told *Sports Illustrated*.[5]

As he continues to go deeper into experimenting how he can get better, Cousins sleeps in a hyperbaric chamber. He is a voracious reader. He continues to seek wisdom and input. After speaking at a conference with former GE CEO Jack Welch, they connected and Welch became a mentor.

The quarterback who has been doubted most of his life by his teams, by fans, by analysts, and by talking heads presses on. His goal has never been money but rather to become the best player—and person—he can be.

"Two of my favorite verses are Colossians 3:23-24," he said. "'Whatever you do, work at it with all your heart, as working for the Lord, not for human masters, since you know that you will receive an inheritance from the Lord as a reward. It is the Lord Christ you are serving.' While I seek to apply this verse to football, I know that football will end one day. Jesus, however, and all who know Him, will live forever. This great truth means I have an identity, a foundation that can never be taken from me."

> *"Things turn out best for people who make the best of the way things turn out."*
>
> **JOHN WOODEN**

TIM HOWARD

When he was 16 years old, Tim Howard had the Superman shield tattooed on his right bicep. Almost 20 years later he looked like the "Man of Steel" on soccer's biggest stage.

Howard became a national hero and the face of U.S. soccer during the 2014 World Cup. In the U.S. team's first-round match against Belgium, Howard was simply remarkable. He broke the World Cup record for most saves in a match with 15. Most of them were of a spectacular, even acrobatic variety—hurtling his body from right to left as Belgium peppered him with shots on goal.

Despite the U.S. team losing in extra time, which knocked them out of the tournament, in the aftermath, Howard was celebrated worldwide, with #ThingsTimHowardCouldSave trending on Twitter and numerous viral meme photos.

Howard has played in more international matches than any goalkeeper of all time for the U.S. men's national team, with more than 100 appearances since his debut in 2002. He was on the bench for the 2006 World Cup, but in 2009 he established himself as starting keeper for the U.S. in international competition and was the backbone of the team for both the 2010 and 2014 World Cups.

He has become a highly recognized figure worldwide—perhaps the most recognized player in U.S. soccer history—a vastly different type of recognition than he experienced during his youth.

When he was growing up in North Brunswick, New Jersey, Howard had behavioral tics that would manifest at any time. His mom, Esther, researched his symptoms and took him to specialists for help. At first she was told her son was hyperactive. But Esther knew it must be more than that, so she persisted. Eventually doctors discovered Howard had Tourette syndrome, a neurological disorder affecting about 3 in every 1,000, which causes repeated, quick movements and sounds they cannot control. It was a difficult diagnosis for a nine-year-old.

"I don't think, quite honestly, answers had much effect on me," Howard said. "I knew something different was going on, and I knew it was stressing me out. It is a very outward condition, so it's not easy to hide. They told my mom what it was, and I just got on with it. I had questions, but I was just trying to get through the day-to-day more than anything. There was always the 'What if?'

"There are just a lot of questions that are very difficult to answer. As a young kid with all those questions, you cannot even begin to put those into words at times, so it feels out of control."

His Tourette's made a somewhat traumatic childhood even more difficult. Howard was the product of an interracial marriage. His father, Matthew, left before Howard could form any memories of him.

"I came from a family of separated parents and an older brother, and things were tough," said Howard. "Money was tight. My parents worked. My mom worked two jobs to make ends meet. She was an awesome inspiration to me at a really young age. You know, she never really complained. She had a lot to complain about, but she never really complained. She put her nose to the grindstone and got it done. I never went to school without shoes. I never went to bed hungry. I certainly could have, but she was a trooper."

With that as a backdrop, adding a condition that was as hard to understand as it was to pronounce caused Howard to withdraw emotionally. He struggled with self-esteem and wondered what his future would be like, especially if the condition became worse.

"I did not experience a lot of peace," Howard said of his childhood.

"But even though my life often seemed chaotic, I knew I could always count on at least one person to provide calm and stability: my grandmother. Nana's sense of peace was so powerful because it came from her faith in the Lord. Through her, God revealed His love for me as well. It wasn't long before I was following in her footsteps. I wanted the same kind of faith and peace she had, and that is exactly what God gave me."

Howard's grandmother was a single mother of five, working multiple jobs with little support. She still made time to put faith first, making sure her children and their children were in church on Sundays. She had an indelible impact upon Howard.

"She was always the glue, the rock that held everything together," Howard said. "That's not easy, but she did it very quietly and very humbly. That was powerful. I think it's more powerful when you don't speak as much and you go about the business of dealing with struggles. What always stood out about my grandmother for me was her compassion. In the midst of any storm, she had so much peace, which clearly came from one source—God."

On Sundays, the entire Howard family, led by Nana, packed into Mount Zion African Methodist Episcopal Church in New Brunswick. While the congregation was made up of mostly lower-income people, Howard noticed that didn't seem to matter to them.

"Everyone was so thankful, appreciative, and praising God for what they did have," he said. "That's pretty impactful for anybody, and I was only a teenager."

Through the support of his grandmother and his own faith, Howard began to see himself differently. A sense of self-respect grew, as did his confidence, which showed as he put more attention on soccer.

He started playing the sport when he was six years old. As he became good enough to be part of a travel team, going across the country for tournaments, his mom did everything necessary to make sure it happened.

"My mom sacrificed her weekends, her own time, lots of money, and traveling all over the East Coast," Howard said. "That was a huge form of encouragement when I look back on it."

With Howard's combination of size and athleticism and supreme hand-eye coordination, he had the skills to be great. As a teen, he met Tim Mulqueen, a coach known for developing goalkeepers. Mulqueen helped elevate Howard's performance, and soon the teen with Tourette's was a highly sought-after and burgeoning legend.

Howard went straight from high school to Major League Soccer, where he was allocated to the New Jersey Metrostars at the age of 19. His rapid rise continued as he quickly became the best goalkeeper in the MLS. He made nine appearances for the U.S. national team, being groomed as the goalkeeper of the future.

Others took notice as well.

In 2003 Howard signed a four-year contract with Manchester United, becoming the first American to play for what is generally considered the world's top sports franchise.

It was an instant culture shock. The blue-collar New Jersey kid was suddenly on the biggest soccer stage in the world, playing before the sport's most knowledgeable fans and against the greatest players in the world. But with the bigger stage came a bigger spotlight and a bigger microscope. Every detail of Howard's life was made public. He was treated like the Beatles—with similar expectations.

"The level of fanaticism," Howard said, "goes far beyond anything we can fathom in America. The fans truly live and die with every win or loss."

Fans created a song for Tim. "Tim Timoney, Tim Timoney, Tim-Tim Teroo…" they would sing while clinking their pints. He was a rock star.

"One of the things I have seen when you have success and fame and money and all the things that come with that in an athletic career is that it's easy to lose focus and not stay grounded and forget about humility," Howard said. "That's the one thing I've always clung tight to—the fact that it's important to me to stay humble. It's important that I don't get carried away with who I think I am or what people tell me I ought to be. For me, that has been the biggest anchor I have had through my faith."

In his first season with Manchester United, Howard registered 16 games without allowing a goal and was named the English Premier League's best keeper by the Professional Footballer's Association. He had a perfect record in 10 of his first 15 appearances during the season.

In 2004 he became the first American to win an FA Cup medal and was voted goalkeeper of the year by the other Premier League players.

Howard moved on to Everton, another EPL team, in 2006, where he stayed through 2016. In 2016 he moved back to the MLS, signing a deal through 2019 with the Colorado Rapids.

Even as he was nearing age 40, he was competing at a high level, still motivated by the challenge that comes with being a goalkeeper.

"It's a hard position," he said. "If a midfielder or forward messes up, there's another chance, another crack at it. When you're a goalkeeper, there is no second chance. If the ball goes behind you, it's a really, really bad thing.

"There's a lot of negativity in terms of criticism and people who say not-so-nice things, and to be able to deal and cope with that has been a challenge. But it's because of my faith that I have been able to stay grounded."

Through all of the pressure situations, public criticism, and high expectations, Howard has been able to keep his Tourette's under control.

"There are different ways to cope with it," Howard said. "There is some medication, but more often than not it's just self-esteem and having positive influences in your life and having very strong, caring, compassionate people around you. For me, I've always been thankful that I have supportive family and friends.

"I wouldn't know life without it, and I am not sure I would want to… My life has been so blessed because of TS. I have been able to reach out to children who have it—hundreds of kids. I've been able to share my story with them and give them some inspiration and hope."

Seeing the positives is a part of Howard's perspective on the entirety of his experience. He recognizes just how unique his journey has been.

"I am blessed to be living a dream," he said. "And yet if it all went away tomorrow, I know I would still have peace. That probably sounds crazy to most people, but that's the kind of peace Christ gives. It is rooted in His love, and it surpasses all understanding," he told the *Huffington Post*.[1]

"The most important thing in my life is Christ. He's more important to me than winning or losing or whether I'm playing or not. Everything else is just a bonus."

> *"Freedom is not procured by a full enjoyment of what is desired, but by controlling that desire."*
>
> **EPICTETUS**

LOLO JONES

» FACTOIDS

She has bachelor's degrees in both economics and Spanish from LSU.

She competed on *Dancing with the Stars* in 2014.

Lolo Jones is an anomaly.

She is a world champion hurdler and a world champion bobsledder. She is a summer Olympian and a winter Olympian. She is a model and a virgin.

In a generation in which sexual purity has been looked upon as outdated and even unenlightened, Jones is a modern example of self-control, even though it hasn't been easy.

"If there are virgins out there, I'm going to let them know that the hardest thing I've ever done in my life—harder than training for the Olympics, harder than graduating from college—has been to stay a virgin before marriage," she told HBO's *Real Sports.*[1]

Jones won three NCAA titles and earned 11 All-American honors while at Louisiana State University in the 60-meter and 100-meter hurdles. She became the first woman ever to win back-to-back indoor championships in the 60-meter hurdles. Lolo won gold at the 2008 and 2010 World Indoor Championships, and she holds the American record in the 60-meter hurdles.

With all her success around the world, Jones has had less than spectacular experiences at the Olympics. She failed to qualify for the

2004 Summer Olympics in Athens, Greece, and found herself wondering about her future. She told her coach she was going to retire, but her heart led her back to keep running.

With limited finances, she held several part-time jobs, including working at Home Depot, waiting tables, and serving as a personal trainer at a gym.

She qualified for the 2008 Beijing games, where she was favored to win the 100-meter hurdles. She led the race on her way to gold but tripped on the second-to-last hurdle and finished in seventh place.

She then had back surgery prior to the 2012 Olympics to correct a tethered spine, which doctors believed was a factor in her long string of injuries. She came back to compete in the 2012 London Olympics, where many felt she would find redemption.

She tweeted about the comeback: "Thank You, Lord, for another chance and for holding me as I waited."

And then tweeted again: "I never have prayed to win a gold medal at Olympics and never will. The Lord is my Shepherd, and I shall not want. May His will be done."

Jones left London disappointed, finishing fourth and off the medal stand again.

"I'll definitely be reading my Bible and trying to grasp the positives and see what God has to teach me from all this," Jones told the press after the finals. "That's the only way I feel I can get rebalanced right now because I am *so* brokenhearted."

In the aftermath of her latest disappointment, Jones explored her options. She had been introduced to bobsledding by U.S. team member Elana Meyers after her fall in Beijing. She devoted herself to training to compete for a spot on the bobsled team.

In 2012 she was named to the U.S. national team as a pusher–brake woman. In her first career World Cup bobsledding competition, Jones and her teammate Jazmine Fenlator placed second.

She then won a gold medal in the mixed-team event at the 2013 World Championships.

After her sudden bobsledding success, she represented the United States at the 2014 Winter Olympics in Sochi, making her one of the few athletes ever to compete in both the summer and winter games. Her team placed a respectable eleventh.

Jones was raised by a single mother in Des Moines, Iowa. Her birth name was Lori, the same as her mother, so she went by Lolo to avoid confusion. She attended eight schools in eight years while her mom often held down two jobs to support her family of six.

When Jones was in third grade, her family moved into the basement of a Salvation Army church.

"My mom would always try to do by any means necessary to make sure that we had what we needed," Jones said. "I definitely do not think I'd be going for this dream had I not seen her pick herself up so many times and keep fighting for us."

When her family was about to make another move, Jones told her mother she was not going. Rather, she wanted to stay in Des Moines to pursue her dream of running track.

Her coach arranged for her to live with four different families so she could attend all four years of high school. These families as well as some of her teachers recognized what Jones could become if given the opportunity. They became active in her life and formed a community of support to help her select the right classes to prepare for college, find part-time jobs, and procure health insurance and other necessities.

The support gave Jones room to grow. She ended up earning a degree at LSU and matured into an elite hurdler.

She also developed her convictions.

After her *Real Sports* revelation in 2012, she became something of a lightning rod. She was the most followed U.S. track and field athlete on Twitter.

"It's just something, a gift I want to give to my husband," Jones told *Real Sports*. "But please understand, this journey has been hard."[2]

Jones says her faith has sustained her through her struggles, and her sister, Angie Jefferson, has provided encouragement all along the way.

"Angie is my reminder from God to stop at never," Jones said.

Jefferson, then a teenager, bought Jones her first running gear, demonstrating her belief in her sister's ability.

"Life was hard because the ghosts of my childhood were still there,"

Jones wrote in an online essay. "But thankfully, so was [Angie]—constantly reminding me there wasn't anything I couldn't overcome and survive with God's help."[3]

Angie now serves as Jones's manager and constant source of support.

Jones acknowledges the very real tension of feeling sexual desire while also remaining committed to abstinence.

"I've had to constantly remind myself, 'When I am weak, He is strong,'" she said. "I'm really telling myself, 'I can't do this in my own strength.' Even the Word says it's not by your strength, it's by God."

"The first and the best victory is to conquer self. To be conquered by self is, of all things, the most shameful and vile."

PLATO

BUBBA WATSON

> **»FACTOIDS**

His name is Gerry Lester Watson Jr. He's named after his father, a Green Beret.

His wife, Angie, played in the WNBA.

He is not your ordinary golfer.

He's left-handed.

He's self-taught.

He carries a hot-pink shafted driver.

He owns a car from the television series *Dukes of Hazzard*.

And his name is Bubba.

But this is no ordinary Bubba. He also is the owner of two Masters championships.

Bubba Watson is the kind of player fans come to a golf tournament to watch. He is one of the PGA Tour's longest hitters, and he has a wide-open, electric personality.

Off the tee, few players can match Watson's powerful swing. In 2007 he had an average drive of 315.2 yards, and he has been known to hit the ball more than 350 yards. His longest drive in professional competition was 442 yards at the WGC-Bridgestone Invitational. He's also capable of generating ball speed up to 194 mph when it comes off the club.

Perhaps it's his six-foot-three, 180-pound frame that provides the torque to make the ball fly. Long and lean and hitting from the left side with a "let 'er rip" type of approach, he definitely draws a crowd when he is at a tee box.

But Watson is more than just a long hitter. He's a great shotmaker who knows how to win.

He made over $1 million in his first year on the PGA Tour. Through 2017 he had collected nine Tour wins and earned over $37 million.

His best two days on the Tour undoubtedly were closing out Masters wins in 2012 and 2014.

But winning is no longer the ultimate for Watson. There was a time in his life when missed shots, errors, and putts that rimmed out elicited angry reactions and raised his blood pressure.

And Watson says an angry Bubba was not a good look or fun to be around.

"I was so wrapped up in 'Why am I not winning?'" Watson said. "It created frustrations in my head and in my life."

Whenever Bubba blew up, he consistently vented his frustration on his caddie, Ted Scott, who at one point had had enough.

"Bubba was never the same person on and off the course, and he was never very happy," Scott told *Sports Spectrum*.[1]

"I knew I was acting immature between the ropes," Watson told *Faith and Friends*. "My caddie finally stepped up and said you're going to have to change or I'm going to quit."[2]

"'If you're going to continue to act like this,'" Scott said to Watson, recalling the conversation for *Sports Spectrum*, "'I just can't work for you. As much as I love you, and I think you're a great player, it's not in the cards to do this.' When Bubba said I was right, I said, 'I am, really?' I totally expected him to say, 'You're fired.'"[3]

"I was having fun off the golf course but not happy on the course," said Watson. "I knew Teddy was right, and what he said hit home. I had to come up with a new mind-set. For him to say that to me, knowing he might lose the income from working for me, that meant a lot for him to step up and say something."

Watson swapped out the uber-stressed attitude with a new approach to the sport. "Bubba Golf" emphasizes playing and having fun on the course.

He credits three people for the change: his caddie, Scott; his trainer, Adam Fisher; and especially his wife, Angie.

"I've really got a good team around me trying to help me succeed," Watson told *Sports Spectrum*. "Not just in golf, but off the golf course, to be a light for Jesus."[4]

Watson's faith is now central to who he is and what he does. Just before teeing off on the final round of the 2014 Masters, Watson tweeted out two Bible verses.

"People always ask 'Why is Bubba different?'" Watson told *Sports Spectrum*. "They're just trying to figure it out."[5]

Watson tweeted before his third round at Augusta in 2014: "The most important thing in my life? Answer after I golf 18 holes with @JustinRose99. #Godisgood."

Later that day he tweeted: "Most important things in my life—1. God 2. Wife 3. Family 4. Helping others 5. Golf."

Watson is a regular at the PGA Tour's weekly Bible study, along with Zach Johnson and Matt Kuchar. During tournament weeks, the group also studies the Bible on Wednesday nights.

"For me, it's a way to get back connected with the Bible and with God and Jesus," Watson said.

Watson grew up being a "good guy." No drinking, no cheating, and no lying.

"I was doing the right things, but I didn't know what that meant," he said.

In his search for truth, Watson found it after some girls in the neighborhood invited him to church. After attending a few times, he realized he had found what he was looking for. He committed his life to Christ. For him, the change was dramatic.

Watson became less focused on his mechanics and more focused on seeing a shot and manufacturing it. *Sports Illustrated* has called him "golf's ultimate feel player."[6]

"I would get so frustrated because I have this competitive fire going on the course," Watson said. "We all have setbacks, but God doesn't give us more than we can handle. So I read my Bible and had key thoughts like *Don't worry about this shot you've blown off the first tee. You have 17 more holes to improve, 6 months to improve.* The Bible is my mental coach now.

"When I play 'Bubba Golf,' I don't worry about what anyone else is doing. It's just me being goofy and creative, havin' fun."

At times, Watson has drawn criticism for being too loose and creative. Some have attacked areas of his game other than his driving skills.

"I listened to my parents, wife, friends, and the Bible instead of them," Watson told *Faith and Friends*. "The Bible says if you're trying to be Christlike, it doesn't matter what others say. You don't need to worry about that. I knew if it was God's plan for me to be on the PGA tour, He would help me do it. It's been working out so far, and it will until He has a different plan for me. I just need to believe in Him."[7]

Watson and Angie have made a priority of using his winnings to help others. They support Birdies for the Brave, which assists military personnel in need; the First Tee, a youth golf and character program; the Ronald McDonald House, helping ill youth; and more.

"Winning is awesome," Watson told *Faith and Friends*. "A pastor friend of mine wanted to start a nondenominational church, and I was able to help him out with that when I came into a lot of prize money really quick! It's an honor to help the organizations I want to be a part of, so coming first in tournaments in January and then May helped me have more money so I can keep helping.

"Don't get me wrong, I'm competitive and want to beat everyone, but the most important thing is being able to help those in need."[8]

That includes helping the two children Watson and Angie have adopted by setting an example.

"I want to be as Christlike as possible," Watson told *CBS This Morning*. "I'll never be perfect. I'm always going to mess up. My whole goal is to be the role model for my son…I want to be the role model, the guy he looks up to and tries to emulate or be better than."[9]

"I expect to pass through the world but once. Any good therefore that I can do, or any kindness I can show to any creature, let me do it now. Let me not defer it, for I shall not pass this way again."

—STEPHEN GRELLET

empathy grace kindness consideration

COMPASSION

tenderness

mercy heart sympathy benevolence charity tenderheartedness

CLAYTON KERSHAW

» FACTOIDS

His catcher in high school was Detroit Lions quarterback Matthew Stafford.

He loves hitting more than pitching.

He is the best pitcher of his generation.

His numbers place him among the finest in the history of baseball.

He is often dominant. At times unhittable.

Watching him work is like watching Rembrandt paint.

With a rare combination of superior stuff and pinpoint control, he rarely gives opposing batters anything to swing at over the heart of the plate.

Yet he gives. In fact, he is one of the most giving athletes of his generation. Because of this, Los Angeles Dodgers left-hander Clayton Kershaw cannot be defined merely by numbers alone.

But the numbers are pretty amazing.

He has a career record of 144-64 through 2017. That's a winning percentage of .692. His lifetime earned run average is a ridiculous 2.36 in a period when the Major League average ERA is two runs higher. His ERA is also the lowest among all starting pitchers in baseball during the live-ball era (which began in 1920). His career walks and hits per innings pitched (WHIP) is also the lowest in the live-ball era. His career hits allowed per nine innings pitched is the second lowest in baseball history.

He became the first pitcher in Major League Baseball history to lead the majors in ERA for four consecutive seasons when he did so from 2011 through 2014. His three seasons with sub-2.00 ERAs is something that has only been done by one other pitcher in the past 50 years.

Pick a number, any number.

- No pitcher has come close to his 15.6 strikeout-to-walk ratio in 2016 when he fanned 172 batters and walked just 11.

- With 12 wins that year (his season was shortened by a back injury), he won more games than batters walked.

- He has won 20 games twice in an era in which the milestone rarely occurs. In fact, it has been achieved just nine times during Kershaw's career.

- He struck out 301 batters in 2015, becoming just the eleventh pitcher to hit that milestone.

Want more?

Three times he has led the NL in wins. Three times he has led the league in strikeouts. Five times he has led the league in ERA.

He has won three Cy Young Awards and was the National League's Most Valuable Player in 2014, becoming just the eleventh pitcher to win the award and the first in the NL in 46 years. He is a seven-time All-Star and has won a Gold Glove Award for fielding excellence.

Oh, and he tossed a no-hitter in 2014, in which he did not surrender a walk and became just the second pitcher ever to strikeout 15 or more in a game in which they did not allow a hit.

Whew!

Kershaw is most often compared to Hall of Famer Sandy Koufax. Both are lefties and both put up their numbers as Dodgers. Yet despite Koufax's brilliance, his dominance was limited to four and a half seasons. Kershaw's current run has lasted *seven* seasons.

When Kershaw made his major league debut in 2008 at age 20, he was the youngest player in baseball. He showed poise beyond his youth, and by his second season, he was already a force at age 21.

In 2017 Kershaw led the Dodgers to the National League pennant and into the World Series for the first time since 1988. They fell one game short to the Houston Astros in one of the most thrilling series in history, but they demonstrated they will be a consistent contender.

"Up there with getting married and having kids, it's right up there with one of the best days of my life," Kershaw said in a press conference. "Winning the World Series is really all that we play this game for. All the individual stuff is great, but at the end of the day, I just want to win a World Series. If we win, I might retire, so I might just call it a career. It's a special thing, and I know I'm not taking that for granted."[1]

Other numbers are important to Kershaw. Like the number of children in Africa who live in need. Or the number of children in Texas who have similar needs. Or the number of dollars he and his wife, Ellen, can give to help change that.

Kershaw and Ellen started Kershaw's Challenge, a nonprofit organization that helps at-risk and homeless children in Los Angeles, Dallas (his hometown), and Lusaka, Zambia. For his efforts, Kershaw received the Roberto Clemente Award in 2012, which is given to the player who "best exemplifies the game of baseball, sportsmanship, community involvement and the individual's contribution to his team." He was 24 at the time of the award.

"Baseball is more than just a passion of mine. It's a platform to do more, to give back to our community, and to make a difference in the world," Kershaw said.

"I obviously love baseball and want to play it as long as I can," Kershaw told the *Dallas Morning News*, "but the foundation work is something that impacts more people's lives in more ways for a longer period of time.[2]

Kershaw created a program within the nonprofit—Kershaw's Challenge: Striking Out to Serve. Through the program, Kershaw and Ellen contribute $100 for every strikeout Kershaw records during the season. Each dollar goes to one of the selected missions. As a result, they have given hundreds of thousands of dollars each year.

"Using God's platform, we don't think of it as philanthropy, but more stewardship," Kershaw said. "Whatever God has given us, we're just a vessel for it. We don't own anything we have. It's all a gift from God, so we're just trying to be good stewards to what He has given us."

The Kershaws have been touched as college, high school, and Little League baseball players have joined the challenge, donating 25 cents or a dollar or more per batter they struck out or per hit they get. Nonathletes partnered too, donating various amounts.

"We all have a platform and a sphere of influence," Kershaw said. "No matter how old you are, you can make a difference right now. I encourage you to create a challenge of your own. Figure out what you are talented at or passionate about and use that to give back to others. As I strike out to serve others this session, I encourage you to also give back in your own unique way.

"Everybody waits for life experiences. Ellen and I, we're just trying to make a difference where we can."

In 2011 Clayton and Ellen traveled to Zambia and saw the need for the at-risk children there. Their hearts were touched. They committed to help build an orphanage, called Hope's Home, for about a dozen children, as well as provide them with education and medical care.

"Our inspiration is a 12-year old girl named Hope," Kershaw said. "She is an HIV orphan who stole our hearts."

To provide a home for Hope and others like her, the Kershaws devoted the proceeds from Kershaw's Challenge to go to projects run by Arise Africa.

Africa was of special interest to the Kershaws because Ellen had been there several times when she was in college and after.

"The first time you hold a Zambian orphan," Ellen told *Sports Spectrum*, "your entire life will be changed because it becomes so personal, so real. The overwhelming blanket of poverty is in this one child, and you realize that if you can only make a difference in this one person's life, that may be what God is calling you to do for your whole existence on earth."[3]

"I learn something every time [we go]," Kershaw told *Sports Illustrated*. "We take it for granted that we get to play. Over there it's more about getting basic needs met. That's something to keep in perspective always."[4]

Africa is not their only point of interest. The Kershaws have partnered with the Peacock Foundation in Los Angeles, an organization that uses rescue animals for therapy for traumatized children; Mercy Street in Dallas, an organization creating transformation through mentoring and community development; and I Am Second, a national media campaign empowering people to live for God and others. They have also helped build a baseball facility for underserved youth in Dallas.

"What I do has a purpose beyond this lifetime," Kershaw said.

And so he finds purpose in the numbers—both on and off the field—in fulfilling what Kershaw believes is a calling: to use baseball as a means to impact others.

"It's a gift. I didn't do anything to deserve that," said Kershaw. "You never know what could happen. Baseball could end tomorrow, but just understanding that God's in control of it, and we're not.

"The prayer I say before I go out there and pitch is not 'God, let me win today' or 'God, help me pitch well.' It's 'God, just be with me.' With all the different people and different cultures and different religions, you can kind of just become one with the crowd. You gotta keep reminding yourself that you're supposed to stand out. You're supposed to be different."

Different he is, indeed. Perhaps even otherworldly.

"Men are only great as they are kind."

ELBERT HUBBARD

KYLE KORVER

»FACTOIDS

His first job was at the Garden Chapel Funeral Home in his hometown in Iowa.

His favorite vacation spot is Turks and Caicos.

Cleveland Cavaliers forward Kyle Korver is considered by many to be one of the greatest shooters in NBA history. In fact, he has been ever since he entered the league in 2003. In his career he's made more than 2,000 three-pointers and holds the NBA record for the highest three-point field goal percentage in a single season at 53.6% in the 2009–10 season.

In January 2018, Korver drained his 2,134th three-pointer, making him the fourth-most prolific three-point shooter in NBA history. Only Ray Allen, Reggie Miller, and Jason Terry are ahead of him on the list. He set the NBA record by hitting a three in 90 consecutive games.

Korver had successful stints in Philadelphia, Utah, Chicago, and Atlanta before being traded to Cleveland during the 2016–17 season. Throughout his career, he has primarily come off the bench to provide a long-range scoring threat, but he is also a top-notch defender.

When the Cavaliers traded for him, they felt he would be a key piece to help them get back to the NBA Finals.

The Cavs paid a hefty price to acquire Korver, sending Mike Dunleavy, Mo Williams, and a protected future first-round pick to Atlanta for what amounted to just five and a half guaranteed months of the six-foot-seven swingman's services.

"[Incredible] sharpshooter and just a great guy," said Cavs star LeBron James of Korver. "Great professional, as you've seen over his career, a guy who's played at a high level for a long time, has championship aspirations. And he has another rocket launcher."[1]

Korver's shooting helped propel the Cavs into the 2017 finals for a rematch against Golden State. The Cavs, however. lost the series, leaving Korver without the championship he had been chasing for 14 years.

Great shooters must have a short memory, forgetting their last shot, whether made or missed, so they can focus on the next shot. Yet one shot in the finals became a hard one for Korver to let go.

It was during Game 3, with the Cavaliers trying not to go down three games to none. They had a two-point lead at home with one minute remaining. James drew Draymond Green to defend him at the top of the three-point arc. He drove into the key and then fired a pass to Korver as he was coming off a screen in the corner. It was a shot Korver has taken and made countless times. In fact, it's the spot where he has the highest shooting percentage for three-pointers in his career. But this time the ball bounced off the front of the rim and into the hands of Kevin Durant, who dribbled to the other end of the floor and buried a three to give the Warriors the lead and eventually the game. They went on to win the series four games to one.

"It felt good when it left my hand," Korver said. "We were up when I shot it. Who knows? They come down and hit a three and change the game. It's one of those things that makes sports awesome. You never know what's going to happen next. Definitely…I don't want to make it a big deal in my head, though. I wish that shot would've gone down for sure."

Even though that shot didn't go down, many others did for Korver during his stay in Cleveland. So the Cavs signed him to a three-year, $22 million deal.

"I was hopeful this was going to work out," he told Bleacher Report. "The better my teammates are, the better I am. I think for me, to be able to come back here and play with 'Bron, and play with these guys, it's an incredible opportunity. When it's all said and done, to say that you played with this group, it's just something you want to take advantage of."[2]

The feeling is mutual toward the player former teammate Kyrie Irving once labeled the "best shooter in the world."

Cavaliers coach Ty Lue calls Korver "the ultimate competitor" and says his movement on the court "creates confusion" for defenses.

James gave him the nickname "Mr. Fourth Korver."

"He makes our team special with what he's able to do and the way he's able to move off the ball," former Cavs guard Dwayne Wade told Bleacher Report. "He never stops moving, and even when he's not making shots, he's still a threat with the defense. They always got to have an eye on him, so it allows other guys to be able to have moments where they can sneak-attack or have a little bit more space on the floor. I know LeBron is the guy and gets the headlines, but to me, Kyle is as important to our success, for sure."[3]

Drafted in the same class as both James and Wade—albeit more than 40 picks after both—Korver found himself chasing a championship in Cleveland with the two future Hall of Famers.

To play through the aches and pains, Korver continuously looked for ways to improve his diet and sleep patterns. And even with his impressive shooting statistics, he is constantly working to become a better shooter.

Playing 15 seasons in the league exceeds Korver's expectations from when he was drafted.

"The goal was always to get to double-digits," Korver told CBS Sports. "When you're younger, you're like, 'Man if I could play double-digits in the NBA, it would be amazing.' I feel incredibly fortunate and blessed to be able to keep doing this…I try to just focus on today. It's been a pattern over my career, and it's probably a good reason why I'm still playing."[4]

Korver's pregame preparation is part routine and part science. About an hour before each game, he goes onto the court and grabs a ball. After taking a few shots to get down the ideal release and rotation, he heads to the top of the three-point line. He stays there, taking passes from an assistant coach, until he hits ten threes. He is perfecting his release and muscle memory.

He then moves to different spots on the court, shooting shot after shot, mimicking in-game moves until he has drilled shots from every spot in his circuit. For close to 15 minutes he launches more than 100 shots.

"I find the shots I think I'm getting in the game," Korver told Bleacher Report. "Those are the shots I try to focus on. Different offenses, different teams. You just want to get your mechanics down. I try to think through everything. Every day you try to find your shot. You try to find the groove you want to be in. It takes a bunch of shots to get there, just waking everything up and finding that groove."[5]

Korver's former coach in Atlanta, Mike Budenholzer, is not surprised by Korver's longevity and success.

"It's a testament to his hard work and sticking to his process," Budenholzer told Bleacher Report. "His off-season training. His in-season training. His attention to detail...He's a special human being, and it translates to what he's been able to do at a high level at his age."[6]

In addition to meticulous preparation on and off the court, Korver's motivation is simple.

"It's the next shot," he said. "I get mad about the last one sometimes, but you have to keep on shooting, keep on believing in what you do. There are a lot more games to come."

One of the opportunities to come, he hopes, will be another shot at a game clincher in the finals. He says he *wants* to have that shot again. "All you can ask for are opportunities, and you go out there and try to make the most of them."

"I love the process of it all," Korver said. "When I sit back and look at my career, you can't appreciate the good moments without having to go through the hard moments. It's a different way of looking through hard times, but you have to have those. The people who have done the greatest things in life usually have the hardest stories of how they got there. I think you just have to understand it's all part of the journey and a part of the process, and you never know what's going to happen next.

"People always ask me, 'What's your highest moment?' and I never know how to answer that question. I hope the best is yet to come. I never like to live in the past. I never say, 'Those were the glory days.' Some people think about that with high school. Some think about it with college or a certain moment. I think, the way I want to live, is the best is yet to come."

Korver's positive outlook stems a great deal from his upbringing in rural Pella, Iowa, a town with a love for basketball and church.

"My dad, grandpa, and a couple of my uncles were pastors, and I grew up with so many godly examples to look up to in addition to them," Korver said. "What a gift that was for me. I don't think a young man could ask for a better gift than an incredible example for life from his father."

Korver's dad, Kevin, and his mom were also standout basketball players at Pella High School and Central College. His mom, Laine, once scored 74 points in a high school game.

The shooting gene was passed down to the next generation. Along with Kyle, his brothers, Kirk, Kaleb, and Klayton, all played Division I basketball.

Korver followed in his parents' footsteps to Pella High School, where his number was retired in 2006. He then played four seasons at Creighton University, earning second-team All-America honors his senior year.

The accolades and accomplishments have never been a priority for Korver. He is more interested in how he can use his platform to make a difference in the lives of others. His caring heart was awakened as a young boy growing up in a rough part of California. He joined his dad on Saturday cleanup projects around the city. By 1988 the elder Korver's "Lookin' Good" program won national recognition. Kyle learned then the value of investing in others.

"To me, service is just part of what you believe," said Korver. "You shouldn't do it because you feel you have to. You shouldn't do it because you feel pressure. You should do it just because it's who you are and who God created you to be."

"It's easy to get caught up in stupid, vain stuff, [like] wearing certain clothes or buying certain cars. How you spend money and what you invest in—those are big questions. It's also easy to start thinking you're more important than you are. But that's why true community is so important to us."

Because of his passion for helping others, Korver launched his own foundation early in his NBA career. The Kyle Korver Foundation is involved in a number of charitable causes to help those in need.

"At the foundation, we believe a grassroots, individualistic approach is the way to enact change," Korver told *Sports Spectrum*. "One child, one family, one class, one school, one neighborhood, one city. That's it."[7]

The foundation has had an impact on every area Korver has played: homeless shelters and schools in urban Philadelphia, home repairs and coat drives in Salt Lake City, coat drives in Chicago, sock drives and accessible home builds in Atlanta. They have also provided shoes for children in India and medical and dental supplies for the needy in South Africa through the NBA's Basketball Without Borders initiative.

"When you can help, it's what you do," he said. "It's not done for reward or because you have to or so others can see. It's done because you can."

The issue that most grabbed Korver's heart is human trafficking. During the 2017 season he decided to do something to bring attention to the problem.

He marked his right hand with a large red X for a game against the New York Knicks. By doing this, Korver joined thousands of people across the country to bring awareness to human trafficking and slavery by joining the End It Movement.

"One day a year, and literally thousands of people across the world, letting people know there's over 27 million slaves in the world today," Korver told the press after the game. "Raising awareness. Just trying—I mean, people hear that number [27 million] and they're like, 'Man, are you serious? I didn't know about that.'

"A lot of people are fighting this fight. That's what these red X's are all about."

Over the course of his NBA career, actions like these have defined Korver. He is known more for his character, integrity, and faith than for his record-setting on-court marksmanship.

"Kyle's one of the most professional, high-character players I've ever been around," said former coach Budenholzer.[8]

"I believe God is seeking all of our hearts, and if we are truly seeking His, He's going to take hold of us," Korver said. "When He does, the roots of our faith will grow deep. That's what makes for a rich life."

JASON WITTEN

»FACTOIDS

He has two dogs, named Tink and Lucy Knox.

When he was drafted, both he and his wife, Michelle, were too young to rent a car in Texas.

Jason Witten is a survivor. In more ways than one.

Before his retirement after the 2017 season to join the *Monday Night Football* booth, the Dallas Cowboys tight end survived 15 seasons at one of the most physically demanding positions in football.

Through the years, Witten has proven to be one of the toughest players in the game, as evidenced by the fact that through the end of the 2017 season he had played 239 consecutive games. Only 11 players in history have longer streaks—5 of which are kickers or punters and none of which are tight ends.

One of the finest at his position in NFL history, Witten ranks fourth on the all-time list of pass catchers in league history, with 1,152 catches through 2017, and he stands second among tight ends.

Witten was one of the few tight ends who is as skilled as a blocker as he is a receiver. Gifted with great hands, he was as sure a target as the game has seen.

He recorded more than 90 receptions in a season four times, with his high being 110 in 2012—an NFL record for tight ends. He has turned 68 of his catches into touchdowns.

He holds the NFL record for most receptions in a single game by a tight end with 18, and he holds the Cowboys franchise records for career receptions and yards, single-game receptions, and consecutive games played.

He has been voted to 11 Pro Bowls and been selected to the All Pro team four times. In 2012 he received the Walter Payton NFL Man of the Year Award, and in 2013 he was honored with the Bart Starr Award.

None of this success was in Witten's sights when he was younger.

He grew up outside Washington, D.C., in a troubled family. Witten's father was abusive, both verbally and physically. He often became violent with Jason, his mother, and his older brothers.

Witten remembers the screaming. He remembers the confusion, the doubt, and the self-condemnation.

"Those heartaches, those cries in your life that you go through, I thought that every kid goes through them," Witten told *Sports Spectrum*. "I knew I didn't have much, but I didn't know there was another side out there. I thought one present for Christmas was the way it is."[1]

"It impacted my childhood a lot," Witten shared on the Cowboys website. "It's tough. My dad is somebody we loved, but on a handful of days it was your worst nightmare. The pain was deep. It was real. It was something we felt. Seeing others go through pain, such as your mom, I can remember being in the bedroom and just thinking, 'When is this going to end?'"[2]

It ended when Witten was 11. His mother, Kim, took the boys and moved to Elizabethton, Tennessee, to live with her parents.

Witten's grandfather, Dave Rider, was a highly successful football coach at the high school. He became a father figure and role model for Witten, and he eventually became his football coach. The Riders ended up filling the role of parents for Witten and his brothers.

Rider was an example of biblical manhood. He taught Witten about responsibility and respect, about a work ethic, and he instilled a sense of discipline. He daily lived what he taught.

"[Dave Rider] was a role model for how to treat other people, how to treat your wife," Witten's wife, Michelle, told *Sports Spectrum*. "It was a respect factor [Jason's] grandfather put in him. It was how to love other people and do things the right way."[3]

Elizabethton High School eventually named their football stadium after Rider because of the example he set for the community.

When Witten was named to his first Pro Bowl in 2004, the first person he called was his grandfather.

Witten's childhood experiences have driven him to reach out to others suffering from abuse. To do so, he launched the Jason Witten SCORE Foundation in 2007. The foundation supports families affected by domestic violence. SCORE stands for support, community, overcome, rebuild, and educate.

"I remember those feelings and those times, and I see kids now, and I can't really relate my level to theirs," Witten said, "but I know what my feelings were, and they'll be there the rest of my life.

"Our first goal with the foundation was leaving a legacy. We all have an opportunity to make an impact while you're playing. I want to use that to set a standard for long after that. When I'm done playing football 10, 15 years down the road, the foundation is still impacting the youth."

The foundation has benefited families that have stories similar to Jason's by helping to place professionally trained male mentors in domestic violence shelters throughout Texas in order to provide the children in these shelters with positive male role models. The hope is that, through these interactions, the children will learn what a proper father figure does, thus helping break the cycle of domestic violence.

In addition, in 2010, the SCORE Foundation launched a domestic violence prevention program called "Coaching Boys into Men" in the high schools in Arlington, Texas, the home of AT&T Stadium, where the Cowboys play. The program trains coaches to educate their players on the dangers of dating violence.

"I'm trying to break the cycle of family violence," Witten told BP Sports.[4]

"My support in stopping domestic violence is unwavering," Witten says on his website. "And as a professional athlete, I believe big, strong, physical men who have the national spotlight, that's our platform, that's our duty to speak out."[5]

Long before the NFL announced the league would take action to stop domestic violence, Witten was already doing something about it.

"It's about being a man and a role model," Witten told BP Sports. "We take in not just the mothers involved [in domestic abuse], but the children affected by it. That's something we're really active in, and also underprivileged children as a whole. God has blessed me enough to do it because of the game I play.

"I just try to provide hope, and say that 'You are beautiful. You are smart.' Provide avenues for these moms to get back on their feet and encourage them that 'your family's going to be okay.'"[6]

Along with the focus on domestic violence, Witten does more to help hurting and struggling individuals and families. The foundation opened Jason Witten Learning Centers at Boys and Girls Club locations in East Dallas and in his hometown of Elizabethton. Witten and Michelle also dedicated the Jason Witten Emergency Waiting Room at the Niswonger Children's Hospital in Johnson City, Tennessee, in 2008. The foundation also operates a youth wellness program called "Play.Move.SCORE" at Boys and Girls Clubs in Dallas and Fort Worth.

In addition, the annual Jason Witten Football Camp, held each June in Elizabethton, has become one of the nation's largest free football camps, with more than 1,000 youth attending from Tennessee and several surrounding states.

Witten has received praise from teammates, coaches, and opponents for all of this work and the role model he has become to so many. They point to the type of husband and father he is now after coming from a violent upbringing.

Because of that example, in 2017 a new college football honor was inaugurated. The Jason Witten Collegiate Man of the Year will be given to the college football player who demonstrates exemplary leadership on and off the field.

"Your legacy as an athlete means a lot, but God has got to have a huge impact on your life," Witten told *Sports Spectrum*. "I think about the way He can use me and what a platform we have as athletes. God doesn't give you this talent just to win titles.

"God's blessed me in so many ways, with my family, and I've just learned so much from Him…Everything I do is out of relationship with Him, and that's what my life's about. Without Jesus, I'm nobody."[7]

NOTES

1. COMMITMENT

Drew Brees

1. Jason Romano, "Drew Brees on Overcoming Obstacles and Trusting God," *Sports Spectrum*, September 14, 2017, https://sportsspectrum.com/sport/football/2017/09/14/drew-brees-overcoming -obstacles-trusting-god/.
2. Romano, "Drew Brees on Overcoming Obstacles and Trusting God."
3. Romano, "Drew Brees on Overcoming Obstacles and Trusting God."

Paul Goldschmidt

1. Scott Boeck, "Paul Goldschmidt, Practically Perfect to D'backs: 'Jesus Christ in a Baseball Uniform,'" *USA Today*, March 27, 2016, https://www.usatoday.com/story/sports/mlb/2016/03/27/paul-goldschmidt-diamondbacks-contract-superstar/82321458/.
2. Tyler Kepner, "Paul Goldschmidt's Teammates Cheer His M.V.P. Campaign," *New York Times*, August 26, 2017, https://www.nytimes.com/2017/08/26/sports/baseball/arizona-diamondbacks-paul-gold schmidt-mvp.html.
3. Scott Boeck, "Paul Goldschmidt, Practically Perfect to D'backs: 'Jesus Christ in a Baseball Uniform.'"
4. Scott Boeck, "Paul Goldschmidt, Practically Perfect to D'backs: 'Jesus Christ in a Baseball Uniform.'"
5. Nick Piecoro, "Baserunning a 'priority' for Diamondbacks' Paul Goldschmidt," *AZcentral*, April 18, 2017, https://www.azcentral.com/story/sports/mlb/diamondbacks/2017/04/19/baserunning -priority-diamondbacks-paul-goldschmidt/100634752/.
6. Scott Boeck, "Paul Goldschmidt, Practically Perfect to D'backs: 'Jesus Christ in a Baseball Uniform.'"
7. Scott Boeck, "Paul Goldschmidt, Practically Perfect to D'backs: 'Jesus Christ in a Baseball Uniform.'"
8. Scott Boeck, "Paul Goldschmidt, Practically Perfect to D'backs: 'Jesus Christ in a Baseball Uniform.'"
9. Ben Reiter, "How Paul Goldschmidt Turned Himself into a Perennial MVP Candidate," *Sports Illustrated*, August 17, 2015, https://www.si.com/mlb/2015/08/19/paul-goldschmidt-arizona-diamond backs-mvp.
10. Gina Maravilla, "D-backs' Goldschmidt shares spiritual side of his private life," azfamily. com, February 23, 2016, http://www.azfamily.com/story/31293588/d-backs-goldschmidt-shares-personal-side-of -his-private-life?clienttype=generic&mobilecgbypass.

David Johnson

1. Greg Bishop, "The X-Man Factor: David Johnson's Freaky-Good Skills at the Core of His Unlikely Rise to Stardom," *Sports Illustrated*, August 31, 2017, https://www.si.com/nfl/2017/08/31/david-johnson-arizona-cardinals-injury-family.
2. Bishop, "The X-Man Factor: David Johnson's Freaky-Good Skills at the Core of His Unlikely Rise to Stardom."
3. Bishop, "The X-Man Factor: David Johnson's Freaky-Good Skills at the Core of His Unlikely Rise to Stardom."

Jenny Simpson

1. Adam Carlson, "Jenny Simpson Makes History Earning U.S.A.'s First-Ever Medal in Women's 1500-Meter," *People*, August 16, 2016, https://people.com/sports/rio-olympics-jenny-simpson-earns -bronze-in-1500m-u-s-a-s-first-medal-in-event/.

2. LEADERSHIP

Case Keenum

1. Dan Pompei, "How Case Keenum Went from Unwanted Free Agent to Leader of the NFC Favorites,"

Bleacher Report, January 11, 2018, http://bleacherreport.com/articles/2753351-how-case-keenum-went-from-unwanted-free-agent-to-leader-of-the-nfc-favorites.

2. Pompei, "How Case Keenum Went from Unwanted Free Agent to Leader of the NFC Favorites."

3. Pompei, "How Case Keenum Went from Unwanted Free Agent to Leader of the NFC Favorites."

4. Chip Scoggins, "The legend of Case Keenum grows exponentially," *Star Tribune*, January 15, 2018, http://www.startribune.com/the-legend-of-case-keenum-grows-exponentially/469307453/.

5. Pompei, "How Case Keenum Went from Unwanted Free Agent to Leader of the NFC Favorites."

6. Pompei, "How Case Keenum Went from Unwanted Free Agent to Leader of the NFC Favorites."

7. Pompei, "How Case Keenum Went from Unwanted Free Agent to Leader of the NFC Favorites."

8. Pompei, "How Case Keenum Went from Unwanted Free Agent to Leader of the NFC Favorites."

9. Megan Bailey, "Vikings QB Case Keenum Grounded in Christian Faith," beliefnet, http://www.beliefnet.com/columnists/idolchatter/2018/01/vikings-qb-case-keenum-grounded-christian-faith.html.

10. Lindsey Young, "Family, Faith & Hidden Heroes Help Case Lead a Huddle," Vikings.com, October 30, 2017, http://www.vikings.com/news/article-1/Family-Faith—Hidden-Heroes-Help-Case-Keenum-Lead-a-Huddle/7f50b137-ef11-4daf-918c-f81e922f6f1a.

11. Bailey, Vikings QB Case Keenum Grounded in Christian Faith."

12. Pompei, "How Case Keenum Went from Unwanted Free Agent to Leader of the NFC Favorites."

13. Justin Adams, "Vikings QB Case Keenum grounded by faith, family, football," *Sports Spectrum*, September 27, 2017, https://sportsspectrum.com/sport/football/2017/09/27/vikings-qb-case-keenum-grounded-faith-family-football/.

Brad Stevens

1. Tim Layden, "Hub Fans Bid Kid…" *Sports Illustrated*, August 26, 2013, https://www.si.com/vault/2013/08/26/106361067/hub-fans-bid-kid.

2. Layden, "Hub Fans Bid Kid…"

3. Layden, "Hub Fans Bid Kid…"

4. Andrew Sharp, "Going Green," *Sports Illustrated*, March 21, 2016, https://www.si.com/nba/2016/03/22/boston-celtics-brad-stevens-danny-ainge-isaiah-thomas-jae-crowder.

5. Sharp, "Going Green."

6. Jay King, "Kyrie Irving tries to explain greatness of Boston Celtics' Brad Stevens: It's like almost bringing college to the NBA," January 12, 2018, http://www.masslive.com/celtics/index.ssf/2018/01/kyrie_irving_tries_to_explain.html.

7. Sharp, "Going Green."

8. Diamond Leung, "Brad Stevens talks about his faith," ESPN.com, May 17, 2011, http://www.espn.com/blog/collegebasketballnation/post/_/id/31020/brad-stevens-talks-about-his-faith.

9. Steven Copeland, "The Way," *Sports Spectrum*, December 20, 2011, https://sportsspectrum.com/tag/brad-stevens-faith/.

10. Steven Copeland, "The Way."

Dabo Swinney

1. David M. Hale, "The Tao of Dabo Swinney," ESPN, December 31, 2017, http://www.espn.com/college-football/story/_/id/21916855/clemson-tigers-dabo-swinney-culture-alabama-crimson-tide-nick-saban-process.

2. Mark Schlabach, "Dabo Swinney overcame pain and poverty to be on the cusp of history," ESPN, Januray 6, 2016, http://www.espn.com/college-football/story/_/id/14519758/dabo-swinney-overcame-pain-poverty-reach-new-heights-clemson.

3. Schlabach, "Dabo Swinney overcame pain and poverty to be on the cusp of history."

4. Schlabach, "Dabo Swinney overcame pain and poverty to be on the cusp of history."

5. Paul Myerberg, "Coaching tree for Clemson's Dabo Swinney begins to grow," USA TODAY SPORTS, 12/23/17, https://www.msn.com/en-us/sports/ncaafb/coaching-tree-for-clemsons-dabo -swinney-begins-to-grow/ar-BBHbWb2.

6. Myerberg, "Coaching tree for Clemson's Dabo Swinney begins to grow."

7. Hale, "The Tao of Dabo Swinney."

8. Hale, "The Tao of Dabo Swinney."

9. Hale, "The Tao of Dabo Swinney."

10. Hale, "The Tao of Dabo Swinney."

11. Hale, "The Tao of Dabo Swinney."

12. Justin Adams, "Clemson head coach Dabo Swinney signs 8-year, $54 million extension," *Sports Spectrum*, August 25, 2017, https://sportsspectrum.com/sport/football/2017/08/25/clemson-head -coach-dabo-swinney-signs-8-year-54-million-extension/.

3. PERSEVERANCE

Simone Biles

1. Mark Zeigler, "Biles wins all-around gold, called 'best ever,'" sandiegotribune.com, August 11, 2016, http://www.sandiegouniontribune.com/sports/olympics/sdut-olympics-simone-biles-gymnatics -all-around-2016aug11-story.html.

2. Kevin Sherrington, "Emotional all-around gold medal moment solidifies Simone Biles as the great-est female gymnast ever," SportsDay, August 2016, https://sportsday.dallasnews.com/other-sports/ olympics/2016/08/11/sherrington-emotional-around-gold-medal-moment-solidifies-simone -biles-as-greatest-female-gymnast-ever.

3. Kevin Sherrington, "As Rio gymnastics end, 'greatest ever' Simone Biles on whole different level than competition," SportsDay, August 2016, https://sportsday.dallasnews.com/other-sports/olym pics/2016/08/16/sherrington-rio-gymnastics-end-greatest-eversimone-biles-whole-different-level -competition.

4. Chrös McDougall, "Mary Lou Retton: Simone Biles 'May Be Most Talented Gymnast' Ever," Team USA, August 24, 2014, https://www.teamusa.org/news/2014/august/24/mary-lou-retton-simone -biles-may-be-most-talented-gymnast-ever.

5. Callum Ng, "Simone Biles: What you need to know," CBC Sports, August 9, 2016, http://www.cbc .ca/m/sports/olympics/rio2016/artistic-gymnastics/instant-profile-simone-biles-1.3714023.

6. Simone Biles, simonebiles.com, http://www.simonebiles.com/.

7. Michael Hardy, "Gold Rush," *Texas Monthly*, July 2016, https://www.texasmonthly.com/the-culture/ simone-biles-olympic-gymnast/.

8. Roland Mechler, "God Works for the Good," Athletes Devotional, February 3, 2018, http://www .athletesdevotional.com/2018/02/03/god-works-for-the-good/.

9. Brian Cazeneuve, "Flipping Awesome," *Sports Illustrated*, August 22, 2016, https://www.si.com/ vault/2016/09/14/flipping-awesome.

10. Cazeneuve, "Flipping Awesome."

11. Christine Thomasos, "Simone Biles on Sharing Christian Faith with Children She Meets," the *Christian Post*, November 26, 2016, https://www.christianpost.com/news/simone-biles-sharing -christian-faith-with-children-171729/.

Abbey D'Agostino

1. Martin Rogers, "Abbey D'Agostino out of 5,000 with torn ACL; her Olympic moment lives on," USA Today, August 17, 2016, https://www.usatoday.com/story/sports/olympics/rio-2016/2016/08/17/ abbey-dagostino-tears-acl-5000/88888662/.

2. Rogers, "Abbey D'Agostino out of 5,000 with torn ACL; her Olympic moment lives on."

3. Rogers, "Abbey D'Agostino out of 5,000 with torn ACL; her Olympic moment lives on."

4. Stacie Fletcher, "When Glorifying God Means Coming in Last Place," Cru.org, August 19, 2016, https://www.cru.org/us/en/communities/athletes/when-glorifying-god-means-coming-in-last -place.html.

Clint Dempsey

1. Clint Dempsey, "Clint Dempsey: Finding Strength in the Lord," *FCA* magazine, June 17, 2014, http://www.fca.org/magazine-story/2014/06/17/clint-dempsey-finding-strength-in-the-lord.

2. AP, "Dempsey closes in on Donovan's US national team goals record," *USA Today*, June 1, 2017, https://www.usatoday.com/story/sports/soccer/2017/06/01/dempsey-closes-in-on-donovans-us -national-team-goals-record/102398746/.

3. AP, "Dempsey closes in on Donovan's US national team goals record."

4. Graham Parker, "Clint Dempsey on His Heart, His Career and Another Chance at a Title," *New York Times*, December 8, 2017, https://www.nytimes.com/2017/12/08/sports/soccer/clint-dempsey -seattle-sounders-mls.html.

Monty Williams

1. Michael Wright, "Monty Williams gives emotional speech at wife's funeral," ESPN.com, February 19, 2016, http://www.espn.com/nba/story/_/id/14803989/monty-williams-oklahoma-city-thunder -gives-emotional-speech-wife-ingrid-williams-funeral.

2. Dave Pond, "Exhibit A," *FCA* magazine, February 26, 2015 http://www.fca.org/magazine-story/ 2015/02/26/exhibit-a.

4. TEAMWORK

Allyson Felix

1. *Christianity Daily*, "Olympic Gold Medalist Allyson Felix: 'Faith Leads My Life,'" August 11, 2016, http://www.christianitydaily.com/articles/8385/20160811/olympic-gold-medalist-allyson-felix -faith-leads-life.htm.

2. *Christianity Daily*, "Olympic Gold Medalist Allyson Felix: 'Faith Leads My Life.'"

Laurie Hernandez

1. Eun Kyung Kim, "Simone Biles on beam upset, Laurie Hernandez's silver: 'I'm so proud of her,'" *Today*, August 16,2016, https://www.today.com/news/simone-biles-beam-upset-laurie-hernandez -s-silver-i-m-t101876.

2. "Laurie Hernandez Biography," the Biography.com website, November 23, 2016, https://www.biog raphy.com/people/laurie-hernandez-080116.

3. Stacie Fletcher, "Gymnast hopes to head to Rio: 'I don't fear the future anymore,'" Cru, July 8, 2016, https://www.cru.org/us/en/communities/athletes/gymnast-hopes-to-head-to-rio-i-dont-fear-the -future-anymore.html.

4. Fletcher, "Gymnast hopes to head to Rio: 'I don't fear the future anymore.'"

5. Fletcher, "Gymnast hopes to head to Rio: 'I don't fear the future anymore.'"

6. Stacie Fletcher, "Laurie Hernandez Inspires at the Olympics," Cru, August 11, 2016, https://stage.cru .org/us/en/communities/athletes/laurie-hernandez-inspires-at-the-olympics.html.

7. Fletcher, "Gymnast hopes to head to Rio: 'I don't fear the future anymore.'"

8. Fletcher, "Gymnast hopes to head to Rio: 'I don't fear the future anymore.'"

Jordy Nelson

1. Tim Layden, "Cream of the Crop," *Sports Illustrated*, December 1, 2014, https://www.si.com/nfl/2014/11/25/green-bay-packers-jordy-nelson-sports-illustrated-cover.

2. Layden, "Cream of the Crop."

5. RESPECT

Kevin Durant

1. Cru.org, "Kevin Durant: Growing Spiritually," Cru.org, https://www.cru.org/us/en/communities/athletes/kevin-durant-growing-spiritually.html.

2. Life.church, "Interview with Kevin Durant and Carl Lentz," Life.church, https://www.life.church/watch/growing-spiritually/.

Jeremy Lin

1. Derrick Battle, "Fil-Lin' in the Blanks on Jeremy Lin," Liberty Champion, February 12, 2012, https://www.liberty.edu/champion/2012/02/editorial-fil-lin-in-the-blanks-on-jeremy-lin/.

2. Howard Beck, "Growing Doubts on Lin's Return to the Knicks," New York Times, July 15, 2012, https://www.nytimes.com/2012/07/16/sports/basketball/jeremy-lin-may-not-return-to-the-knicks.html?_r=0.

3. Kurt Badenhausen, "Time Magazine Picks Jeremy Lin For Cover After Five Games," *Forbes*, February 17, 2012, https://www.forbes.com/sites/kurtbadenhausen/2012/02/17/time-magazine-picks-jeremy-lin-for-cover-after-five-games/#62e8cf962c99.

4. Brian Mahoney, "David Stern: Nothing Like Frenzy Created by Jeremy Lin," NBCMiami.com, February 23, 2012, https://www.nbcmiami.com/news/sports/David-Stern-Nothing-Like-Frenzy-Created-by-Jeremy-Lin-140241563.html.

5. George Henn, "Linsanity to the Extreme," Pressreader, July 15, 2012, https://www.pressreader.com/usa/new-york-daily-news/20120715/283480728288255.

Simone Manuel

1. Faith Karimi, "Simone Manuel: 5 things to know about US swimmer who made history," CNN, August 12, 2016, https://edition.cnn.com/2016/08/12/sport/simone-manuel-olympics-history/index.html.

2. Faith Karimi, "Simone Manuel: 5 Things to know about US swimmer who made history."

3. Karimi, "Simone Manuel: 5 Things to know about US swimmer who made history."

Jordan Spieth

1. Scott Michaux, "Spieth's career forged with magic moments," *The Augusta Chronicle*, April 2, 2016, http://www.augusta.com/masters/story/news/spieth%E2%80%99s-career-forged-magic-moments.

2. Scott Michaux, "Spieth's career forged with magic moments."

3. Scott Michaux, "Spieth's career forged with magic moments."

4. Scott Michaux, "Jordan Speith's 2015 is comparable to best years in gold history," *The Augusta Chronicle*, April 6, 2016, http://www.jacksonville.com/article/20160406/SPORTS/801246135.

5. Scott Michaux, "Star of Spieth family is Ellie," *The Augusta Chronicle*, March 20, 2016, http://www.augusta.com/masters/story/news/star-spieth-family-ellie.

6. Michaux, "Star of Spieth family is Ellie."

6. INTEGRITY

Marcus Mariota

1. Greg Bishop, "2 Oregon," *Sports Illustrated*, December 29, 2014, https://www.si.com/vault/2014/12/29/106697834/2-oregon.

2. Bishop, "2 Oregon."

3. Chelsea Howard, "Titans QB Marcus Mariota played through a quad injury vs. Patriots," The Sporting News, January 14, 2018, http://www.sportingnews.com/nfl/news/patriots-titans-marcus -mariota-injury-quad-playoffs-afc/z5sm2ee98smr1e4gtijgiyqri.

4. Terry McCormick, "Mariota Finds His Swagger, Giving Titans Fans Hope for 2nd-Round Playoff Win," Memphis Daily News, January 12, 2018, https://www.memphisdailynews.com/news/2018/ jan/12/mariota-finds-his-swagger-giving-titans-fans-hope-for-rare-second-round-playoff-win/.

5. Austin American-Statesman, "Mariota," *pressreader*, January 11, 2018, https://www.pressreader.com/ usa/austin-american-statesman/20180111/281943133282052.

6. McCormick, "Mariota Finds His Swagger, Giving Titans Fans Hope for 2nd-Round Playoff Win."

7. FCA Staff, "In His Own Words: Marcus Mariota," *FCA* magazine, January 12, 2015, http://www .fca.org/magazine-story/2015/01/12/in-his-own-words-marcus-mariota.

Maya Moore

1. Maya Moore, "My Faith Journey," Athletes in Action.org, October 21, 2016, https://athletesinaction .org/quickhits/maya-moore-faith-journey?adbsc=social_20170310_1372841&adbid=84023455369 6440320&adbpl=tw&adbpr=20595832#.WrmUHIIh0nO.

2. Joshua Cooley, "Champion for Change," *FCA Magazine*, April 13, 2017, https://www.fca.org/ magazine-story/2017/04/13/champion-for-change.

3. Justin Adams, "Maya Moore named Sports Illustrated's Performer of the Year," *Sports Spectrum*, November 30, 2017, https://sportsspectrum.com/sport/basketball/2017/11/30/lynx-maya-moore -named-sports-illustrateds-performer-year/.

Benjamin Watson

1. Justin Adams, "How Romans 8:28 sparked Benjamin Watson's return form Achilles Injury," *Sports Spectrum*, November 16, 2017, https://sportsspectrum.com/sport/football/2017/11/16/romans-828 -sparked-benjamin-watsons-return-achilles-injury/.

2. Benjamin Watson, TheBenjaminWatson.com, http://www.thebenjaminwatson.com/.

3. Watson, TheBenjaminWatson.com.

4. Jason Romano, "New Podcast: Benjamin Watson, Baltimore Ravens Tight End," *Sports Spectrum Podcast*, June 16, 2017, https://sportsspectrum.com/sports-spectrum-podcast/2017/06/16/new-podcast -benjamin-watson-baltimore-ravens-tight-end/.

5. Justin Adams, "How Christianity Influences Benjamin Watson's Worldview," *Sports Spectrum,* August 18, 2017, https://sportsspectrum.com/sport/football/2017/08/18/christianity-influences-benjamin -watsons-worldview/.

7. RESPONSIBILITY

Steph Curry

1. Rick Reilly, "One hot Curry," ESPN, April 26, 2013, http://www.espn.com/espn/story/_/ id/9207333/stephen-curry-big-shot.

2. Brett Honeycutt, "In the News: Stephen Curry," *Sports Spectrum*, July 23, 2015, https://sportsspec trum.com/sport/basketball/2015/07/23/in-the-news-stephen-curry/.

3. Joshua Cooley, "The Revolution," *FCA* magazine, April 29, 2016, https://www.fca.org/magazine -story/2016/04/29/the-revolution.

4. Cooley, "The Revolution."

5. Reilly, "One hot Curry."

6. Cooley, "The Revolution."

7. Cooley, "The Revolution."

8. Rick Reilly, "Net Gain," ESPN, August 6, 2013, http://www.espn.com/nba/story/_/id/9543252/stephen-curry-hands-mosquito-nets-prevent-malaria-tanzania.

9. Stephen Copeland, "Stephen Curry—The Year That Changed Him," *Sports Spectrum*, June 8, 2018, https://sportsspectrum.com/sport/basketball/2018/06/08/from-the-archives-stephen-curry-the-year-that-changed-him/.

Maya DiRado

1. Morgan Lee, with reporting by Dorcas Cheng-Tozun, "Meet the Rio Olympians Who Put God Before Gold," *Christianity Today*, August 5, 2016, https://www.christianitytoday.com/ct/2016/august-web-only/meet-rio-olympians-who-put-god-before-gold.html.

2. Barry Svrluga, "Maya DiRado could have a long career in swimming, but she doesn't want one," *Washington Post*, August 5, 2016, https://www.washingtonpost.com/sports/olympics/maya-dirado-could-have-a-long-career-in-swimming-but-she-doesnt-want-one/2016/08/05/4cf6203c-5aff-11e6-9aee-8075993d73a2_story.html?utm_term=.53887ae150e0.

3. Dorcas Cheng-Tozun, "Medal-Winning Swimmer Maya DiRado: My Faith Frees Me to Dream Big," *Christianity Today*, August 11, 2016, http://www.christianitytoday.com/ct/2016/august-web-only/olympic-swimmer-maya-dirado-faith-freed-me-to-dream-big.html.

4. Svrluga, "Maya DiRado could have a long career in swimming, but she doesn't want one."

Jrue and Lauren Holiday

1. Jeff Duncan, "Jrue Holiday to miss start of season as pregnant wife Lauren Holiday faces brain surgery," *New Orleans Times-Picayune*, September 4, 2016.

2. Duncan, "Jrue Holiday to miss start of season as pregnant wife Lauren Holiday faces brain surgery."

Daniel Murphy

1. Ben Reiter, "The House of Murph," *Sports Illustrated*, November 2, 2015, https://www.si.com/vault/2016/02/11/house-murph.

2. Drew Van Esselstyn, "A Slugger's Story," *FCA* magazine, March 1, 2017, http://www.fca.org/magazine-story/2017/03/01/a-sluggers-story?utm_source=qa&utm_medium=link&utm_content=17murphyqa.

3. Van Esselstyn, "A Slugger's Story."

4. Van Esselstyn, "A Slugger's Story."

5. Van Esselstyn, "A Slugger's Story."

6. Reiter, "The House of Murph."

7. *FCA* magazine's exclusive interview with MBL slugger Daniel Murphy, July 10, 2017, *FCA* magazine, http://www.fca.org/magazine-story/2017/07/10/fca-magazines-exclusive-interview-with-mlb-all-star-daniel-murphy.

8. Van Esselstyn, "A Slugger's Story."

Carson Wentz

1. Jason Romano, "Carson Wentz—One Year Later," *Sports Spectrum*, April 27, 2017, https://sportsspectrum.com/featured-article-homepage/2017/04/27/carson-wentz-one-year-later/.

2. Romano, "Carson Wentz—One Year Later."

3. Romano, "Carson Wentz—One Year Later."

4. Evan Grossman, "Wentz shares his love for Haiti," *New York Daily News*, January 14, 2018, https://www.pressreader.com/usa/new-york-daily-news/20180114/282162176619479.

8. SELF-CONTROL

Derek Carr

1. Derek Carr, "Derek Carr," The Increase, http://theincrease.com/author/derekcarr/.

2. Derek Carr, "Derek Carr," The Increase, http://theincrease.com/author/derekcarr/.

3. Scott Bair, "Carr Talk," NBCSports.com, http://sportsworld.nbcsports.com/derek-carr-oakland-raiders-season-preview/.

4. Bair, "Carr Talk."

5. Bair, "Carr Talk."

6. Carr, "Derek Carr."

7. Carr, "Derek Carr."

Kirk Cousins

1. Charlene Aaron & Jackson Harris, "Faith on the Field: Kirk Cousins—NFL's Servant Leader," CBN News, December 26, 2015, https://www1.cbn.com/cbnnews/us/2015/December/Faith-on-the-Field-Kirk-Cousins-NFLs-Servant-Leader.

2. Jason Romano, "Redskins QB Kirk Cousins keeps Bible verse in his locker as reminder," *Sports Spectrum*, September 28, 2017, https://sportsspectrum.com/sport/football/2017/09/28/redskins-qb-kirk-cousins-keeps-bible-verse-locker-reminder/.

3. Aaron May, "Kirk Cousins," *Sports Spectrum*, April 19, 2012, https://sportsspectrum.com/featured-article-homepage/2012/04/19/kirk-cousins-ncaa-football-closeup/.

4. Beyond the Ultimate, "Kirk Cousins," 2012, http://beyondtheultimate.com/athlete/Kirk-Cousins.

5. Greg Bishop, "Geek? Yeah. So?" Sports Illustrated, November 29, 2017, https://www.si.com/nfl/2017/11/29/kirk-cousins-washington-redskins-quarterback.

Tim Howard

1. Liz Waid, Colin Lowther, "Tim Howard: Football Role Model", *Spotlight*, June 9, 2014, https://spotlightenglish.com/listen/tim-howard-football-role-model.

Lolo Jones

1. HBO Real Sports, "Lolo Jones: Until Marriage," HBO Real Sports, May 21, 2012, https://www.youtube.com/watch?v=h_SRO9mpt4Y.

2. HBO Real Sports, "Lolo Jones: Until Marriage."

3. Catherine Newhouse, "Why Lolo Jones Is for Real," *UrbanFaith*, August 7, 2012, https://urbanfaith.com/2012/08/why-lolo-jones-is-for-real.html/.

Bubba Watson

1. Art Stricklin, "Touring Together: Inside Bubba Watson and caddy Ted Scott's unique relationship," *Sports Spectrum*, Winter 2016, https://sportsspectrum.com/features/2015/10/10/touring-together-inside-bubba-watson-and-caddy-ted-scotts-unique-relationship/.

2. Trevor Freeze, "Masters Winner Bubba Watson on 'Showing the Light,'" Billy Graham Evangelistic Association, April 11, 2014, https://billygraham.org/story/bubba-watson-showing-the-light/.

3. Stricklin, "Touring Together: Inside Bubba Watson and caddy Ted Scott's unique relationship."

4. Freeze, "Masters Winner Bubba Watson on 'Showing the Light.'"

5. Freeze, "Masters Winner Bubba Watson on 'Showing the Light.'"

6. Michael Bamberger, "The Sixth Sense: Bubba Watson is golf's ultimate feel player," *Golf*, November 10, 2011, http://www.golf.com/tour-and-news/sixth-sense-bubba-watson-golfs-ultimate-feel-player.

7. Jayne Thurber-Smith, "Teed Off," *Salvationist*, April 14, 2014, https://salvationist.ca/articles/2014/04/teed-off/.

8. Thurber-Smith, "Teed Off."

9. Alison Moore, "Bubba Watson, two-time Masters Golf Tournament winner, talks faith and family," Deseret News Family, April 17, 2014, https://www.deseretnews.com/article/865601217/Bubba-Watson-two-time-Masters-Golf-Tournament-winner-talks-faith-and-family.html.

Clayton Kershaw

1. Tom Musick, "Los Angeles Dodgers: Clayton Kershaw, regular-season star, savors postseason success," The Sports Xchange, October 20, 2017, https://www.upi.com/Los-Angeles-Dodgers-Clayton-Kershaw-regular-season-star-savors-postseason-success/7631508511078/.

2. Gerry Fraley, "Full Heart," Dallas Morning News, December 25, 2014.

3. The Increase Baseball, "Striking Out to Serve," April 5, 2016, http://theincreasebaseball.com/featured-articles/striking-out-to-serve/.

4. Dan Patrick, "Just My Type," *Sports Illustrated*, August 25, 2014, https://www.si.com/vault/2014/08/25/106626726/just-my-type.

Kyle Korver

1. Scott Sargent, "NBA Finals Failure Fueling Kyle Korver's First Full Season in Cleveland," Bleacher Report, December 19, 2017, http://bleacherreport.com/articles/2747904-nba-finals-failure-fueling-kyle-korvers-first-full-season-in-cleveland.

2. Sargent, "NBA Finals Failure Fueling Kyle Korver's First Full Season in Cleveland."

3. Sargent, "NBA Finals Failure Fueling Kyle Korver's First Full Season in Cleveland."

4. James Herbert, "Kyle Korver Q&A: Cavaliers veteran sniper on the secrets of staying sharp in Year 15," CBS Sports, November 14, 2017, https://www.cbssports.com/nba/news/kyle-korver-q-a-cavaliers-veteran-sniper-on-the-secrets-of-staying-sharp-in-year-15/.

5. Sargent, "NBA Finals Failure Fueling Kyle Korver's First Full Season in Cleveland."

6. Sargent, "NBA Finals Failure Fueling Kyle Korver's First Full Season in Cleveland."

7. Dave Pond, "On Target," *FCA* magazine, January 5, 2015, https://www.fca.org/magazine-story/2015/01/05/on-target.

8. Pond, "On Target."

Jason Witten

1. "10 things you might not know about Jason Witten, like the evolution of his Tony Romo bromance," *Sportsday*, https://sportsday.dallasnews.com/dallas-cowboys/cowboys/2018/02/25/10-things-might-know-cowboys-te-jason-witten-including-bromance-tony-romo-started.

2. Matthew Connor, "Once a victim, Jason Witten now fights to end domestic violence," https://thelandryhat.com/2015/11/14/jason-witten-fights-domestic-violence/.

3. Todd Archer, "Family Matters to Cowboys' Jason Witten," *The Dallas Morning News*, February 6, 2008, https://utsports.com/news/2008/2/6/Family_matters_to_Cowboys_Jason_Witten.aspx.

4. Joshua Cooley, "Childhood experience moves Cowboys' Witten to help domestic abuse victims," BP Sports, February 24, 2009, http://www.bpsports.net/bpsports.asp?ID=6021.

5. Jason Witten, JasonWitten82.com, http://jasonwitten82.com/.

6. Connor, "Once a victim, Jason Witten now fights to end domestic violence."

7. Jason Romano, "Jason Witten—Sports Spectrum Quotable," *Sports Spectrum*, August 21, 2017, https://sportsspectrum.com/quotables/2017/08/21/jason-witten-sports-spectrum-quotable/.